Presented to

_____

By

_____

On the Occasion of

_____

Date

_____

365
ONE-MINUTE MEDITATIONS

HELEN STEINER RICE

FROM THE INSPIRING VERSE OF AMERICA'S BEST-LOVED POET

365
ONE-MINUTE MEDITATIONS

HELEN STEINER RICE

FROM THE INSPIRING VERSE OF AMERICA'S BEST-LOVED POET

BARBOUR
PUBLISHING

A Minute a Day Can Change Your Life

We're all busy and pressed for time. But somewhere in our daily schedule, there must be at least sixty free seconds. Look for the open minute and fill it with this book. *365 One-Minute Meditations: Helen Steiner Rice* provides a quick but powerful reading for every day of the year, promising real spiritual impact. Each day's entry features a carefully selected verse from God's Word, along with a poem from America's best-loved poet.

Helen Steiner Rice (1900–1981) worked as a greeting card editor before she began writing the countless inspirational poems that have been a favorite of readers for decades. This book is drawn from Rice's beautiful verse, overflowing with encouragement for your spirit. If you're seeking a spiritual lift, try *365 One-Minute Meditations: Helen Steiner Rice*. You'll only need a minute a day—but the benefits could be life-changing.

BEGINNINGS

Thou crownest the year with thy bounty.

PSALM 65:11 RSV

What will you do
With this year that's so new?
The choice is yours—
God leaves that to you!

2

JANUARY

A LIFETIME OF FAVOR

Sing praises to the LORD, O you his saints,
and give thanks to his holy name. For his anger is
but for a moment, and his favor is for a lifetime.

PSALM 30:4–5 RSV

If you meet God in the morning
And ask for guidance when you pray,
You will never in your lifetime
Face another hopeless day.

Helen Steiner Rice

3
JANUARY

BRIGHT TOMORROWS

I will sing of your love and justice;
to you, O LORD, I will sing praise.

PSALM 101:1 NIV

God has told us that nothing can sever
A life He created to live forever.
So let God's promise soften our sorrow
And give us new strength
    for a brighter tomorrow.

One-Minute Meditations

JANUARY

GOD'S SOVEREIGN HAND

*"Both riches and honor come from thee, and thou rulest
over all. In thy hand are power and might; and in
thy hand it is to make great and to give strength
to all. And now we thank thee, our God,
and praise thy glorious name."*

1 CHRONICLES 29:12–13 RSV

Accept what the new year brings,
Seeing the hand of God in all things,
And as you grow in strength and grace,
The clearer you can see God's face.

Helen Steiner Rice

GATEWAY TO JOY

Sing unto the LORD; for he hath done excellent things: this is known in all the earth.

ISAIAH 12:5 KJV

Birthdays are the gateway to
An endless life of joy for you
If you but pray from day to day
That He will show you the truth and the way.

No Unmet Needs

*"The Lord will guide you always;
he will satisfy your needs."*

ISAIAH 58:11 NIV

God only answers our pleadings
When He knows that our wants fill a need,
And whenever our will becomes His will,
There is no prayer that God does not heed!

DAILY RENEWAL

Create in me a clean heart, O God,
and put a new and right spirit within me.

PSALM 51:10 RSV

You are ushering in another day,
Untouched and freshly new,
So here I come to ask You, God,
If You'll renew me, too.

One-Minute Meditations

8

JANUARY

ALWAYS NEAR

*The LORD is near to all who call upon him,
to all who call upon him in truth.*

PSALM 145:18 RSV

Just keep on smiling
Whatever betides you,
Secure in the knowledge
God is always beside you.

Helen Steiner Rice

LOVED AND ACCEPTED

*For God so loved the world, that he gave his only
begotten Son, that whosoever believeth in him
should not perish, but have everlasting life.*

JOHN 3:16 KJV

God asks for no credentials—
　　He accepts us with our flaws.
He is kind and understanding
　　and He welcomes us because
We are His erring children
　　and He loves us, every one,
And He freely and completely forgives
　　all that we have done.

SUPERNATURAL STRENGTH

I can do all things because Christ gives me the strength.

PHILIPPIANS 4:13 NLV

God has given us the answers,
    which too often go unheeded,
But if we search His promises,
    we'll find everything that's needed
To lift our faltering spirits
    and renew our courage, too,
For there's absolutely nothing
    too much for God to do.

Helen Steiner Rice

II
JANUARY

FOSTER A FORGIVING SPIRIT

*Bear with each other and forgive whatever
grievances you may have against one another.
Forgive as the Lord forgave you.*

COLOSSIANS 3:13 NIV

When God forgives us, we, too, must forgive
And resolve to do better each day that we live
By constantly trying to
    be like Him more nearly,
And trust in His wisdom
    and love Him more dearly.

MAKE TIME TO MEDITATE

*I will meditate on all your works and
consider all your mighty deeds.*

PSALM 77:12 NIV

Let us plan with prayerful care
    to always allocate
A certain portion of each day
    to be still and meditate.

Open Eyes, Open Heart

*God looks down from heaven upon the
sons of men to see if there are any that
are wise, that seek after God.*

PSALM 53:2 RSV

It's a wonderful world and it always will be
If we keep our eyes open and focused to see
The wonderful things we are capable of
When we open our hearts
     to God and His love.

ALWAYS THANKFUL

*Giving thanks always for all things unto God and the
Father in the name of our Lord Jesus Christ.*

EPHESIANS 5:20 KJV

We rob our own lives much more than we know
When we fail to respond or in any way show
Our thanks for the blessings
    that daily are ours—
The warmth of the sun,
    the fragrance of flowers,
For the joy of enjoying
    and the fullness of living
Are found in the heart
    that is filled with thanksgiving.

Helen Steiner Rice

15
JANUARY

RELEASE YOUR BURDENS—PRAY!

*Be careful for nothing; but in every thing by prayer
and supplication with thanksgiving let your
requests be made known unto God.*

PHILIPPIANS 4:6 KJV

God only asks us to do our best—
Then He will take over and finish the rest. . .
So when you are tired, discouraged, and blue,
There's always one door that is opened to you,
And that is the door to the house of prayer,
And you'll find God waiting
     to meet you there.

BITTER AND SWEET

He who is sated loathes honey, but to one who is hungry everything bitter is sweet.

PROVERBS 27:7 RSV

Everything is by comparison,
Both the bitter and the sweet,
And it takes a bit of both of them
To make our lives complete.

Our Father's World

*The eyes of the LORD are in every place,
keeping watch on the evil and the good.*

PROVERBS 15:3 RSV

Thank You, God, for the beauty
Around me everywhere,
The gentle rain and glistening dew,
The sunshine and the air.

NOTHING NEW

What has been will be again,
what has been done will be done again;
there is nothing new under the sun.

ECCLESIASTES 1:9 NIV

There is nothing that is new
Beneath God's timeless sun,
And present, past, and future
Are all molded into one.

Helen Steiner Rice

19 JANUARY

DO UNTO OTHERS. . .

*"Whatever you wish that men would do to you,
do so to them; for this is the law and the prophets."*

MATTHEW 7:12 RSV

Great is our gladness
To serve God through others,
For our Father taught us
We are all sisters and brothers.

CAST YOUR CARES

*Casting all your care upon him;
for he careth for you.*

1 PETER 5:7 KJV

When life becomes a problem
    much too great for us to bear,
Instead of trying to escape,
    let us withdraw in prayer—
For withdrawal means renewal
    if we withdraw to pray
And listen in the quietness
    to hear what God will say.

Helen Steiner Rice

21
JANUARY

LIVE TO GIVE

*[You] should give much to those
in need and be ready to share.*

1 TIMOTHY 6:18 NLV

Every day is a reason for giving
And giving is the key to living. . .
So let us give ourselves away,
Not just today but every day.

LOSSES INTO GAIN

I am poor and needy; yet the Lord thinketh upon me:
thou art my help and my deliverer.

PSALM 40:17 KJV

When one sheds a teardrop
    or suffers loss in vain,
God is always there to turn
    our losses into gain. . .
And every burden born today
    and every present sorrow
Are but God's happy harbingers
    of a joyous, bright tomorrow.

Helen Steiner Rice

23
JANUARY

WAITING. . .

May integrity and uprightness preserve me,
for I wait for thee.

PSALM 25:21 RSV

If when you ask for something
God seems to hesitate,
Never be discouraged—
He is asking you to wait.

24

JANUARY

BE RADIANT!

I sought the LORD, and he answered me,
and delivered me from all my fears.
Look to him, and be radiant.

PSALM 34:4–5 RSV

You'll find when you smile,
Your day will be brighter,
And all of your burdens
Will seem so much lighter.

Helen Steiner Rice

25
JANUARY

DAILY WONDERS

Thou are the God who workest wonders,
who has manifested thy might among the peoples.

PSALM 77:14 KJV

Each day there are showers of blessings
Sent from the Father above,
For God is a great, lavish giver,
And there is no end to His love.

26
JANUARY

OUR STRONGHOLD

*The LORD is my rock, and my fortress, and my deliverer,
my God, my rock, in whom I take refuge, my shield,
and the horn of my salvation, my stronghold.*

PSALM 18:2 RSV

God's love is like an anchor
When the angry billows roll—
A mooring in the storms of life,
A stronghold for the soul!

Helen Steiner Rice

27
JANUARY

HAVEN OF GOD'S LOVE

*Then they were glad because they had quiet,
and he brought them to their desired haven.*

PSALM 107:30 RSV

God's love is like a beacon
Burning bright with faith and prayer,
And through the changing scenes of life
We can find a haven there.

MAKING IT PERSONAL

I have called thee by thy name; thou art mine.

ISAIAH 43:1 KJV

Life is a sojourn here on earth
Which begins the day God gives us birth.
We enter this world from the great unknown,
And God gives each spirit a form of its own.

Helen Steiner Rice

STRENGTH FOR THE DAY

*My grace is sufficient for thee:
for my strength is made perfect in weakness.*

2 CORINTHIANS 12:9 KJV

God did not promise sun without rain,
Light without darkness or joy without pain.
He only promised strength for the day
When the darkness comes
and we lose our way.

OUR REFUGE

Yea, though I walk through the valley of the shadow of death, I will fear no evil: for thou art with me; thy rod and thy staff they comfort me.

PSALM 23:4 KJV

The Lord is our salvation
    and our strength in every fight,
Our redeemer and protector,
    our eternal guiding light.
He has promised to sustain us,
    He's our refuge from all harms,
And underneath this refuge
    are the everlasting arms.

HEAVENLY REWARDS

*Remember that the Lord will reward
each one of us for the good we do.*

EPHESIANS 6:8 NLT

At this time may God grant you
Special gifts of joy and cheer
And bless you for the good you do
For others through the year.

SHIELD OF PROTECTION

Every word of God proves true;
he is a shield to those who take refuge in him.

PROVERBS 30:5 ESV

God, be my resting place and my protection
In hours of trouble, defeat, and dejection;
May I never give way to self-pity and sorrow;
May I always be sure of a better tomorrow.

Helen Steiner Rice

2
FEBRUARY

NEW LIFE

*For this slight momentary affliction is preparing for us
an eternal weight of glory beyond all comparison. . .
for the things that are seen are transient, but the
things that are unseen are eternal.*

2 CORINTHIANS 4:17–18 RSV

Little brooks and singing streams,
    icebound beneath the snow,
Begin to babble merrily
    beneath the sun's warm glow,
And all around on every side
    new life and joy appear
To tell us nothing ever dies
    and we should have no fear.

No Place for Pride

*Pride goes before destruction,
and a haughty spirit before a fall.*

PROVERBS 16:18 RSV

Uncover before me my weakness and greed
And help me to search deep inside
So I may discover how easy it is
To be selfishly lost in my pride.

Helen Steiner Rice

4
FEBRUARY

HOPE'S RAINBOW

*We can rejoice, too, when we run into problems
and trials, for we know that they help us develop
endurance. And endurance develops strength
of character, and character strengthens
our confident hope of salvation.*

ROMANS 5:3–4 NLT

The rainbow is God's promise
   of hope for you and me,
And though the clouds hang heavy
   and the sun we cannot see,
We know above the dark clouds
   that fill the stormy sky
Hope's rainbow will come shining through
   when the clouds have drifted by.

HOPE IN GOD

*Why am I discouraged? Why is my heart so sad?
I will put my hope in God! I will praise
him again—my Savior and my God!*

PSALM 42:11 NLT

Meet Him in the morning
    and go with Him through the day
And thank Him for His guidance
    each evening when you pray—
And if you follow faithfully
    this daily way to pray,
You will never in your lifetime
    face another hopeless day.

Helen Steiner Rice

6

FEBRUARY

HOUSE OF PRAYER

*Then shall ye call upon me, and ye shall go and
pray unto me, and I will hearken unto you.*

JEREMIAH 29:12 KJV

The house of prayer is no farther away
Than the quiet spot where you kneel and pray.
For the heart is a temple when God is there
As we place ourselves in His loving care.

SOUL GROWTH

*For it is God which worketh in you both
to will and to do of his good pleasure.*

PHILIPPIANS 2:13 KJV

Help us, dear God, to choose between
The driving forces that rule our routine
So we may make our purpose and goal
Not power and wealth
   but the growth of our souls. . .
And give us strength and drive and desire
To raise our standards and ethics higher,
So all of us and not just a few
May live on earth as You want us to.

WALK IN LOVE

*As you have heard from the beginning,
his command is that you walk in love.*

2 JOHN 1:6 NIV

Sometimes when faith is running low
And I cannot fathom why things are so,
I walk among the flowers I grow
And learn the answers to all I would know.

NO NEED FOR FEAR

The LORD is my light and my salvation;
whom shall I fear?

PSALM 27:1 RSV

After the clouds, the sunshine;
After the winter, the spring;
After the shower, the rainbow—
For life is a changeable thing.

Helen Steiner Rice

10
FEBRUARY

GOD OUR SOUL CULTIVATOR

It is the hard-working farmer who ought
to have the first share of the crops.

2 TIMOTHY 2:6 RSV

God never plows in the soul of man
Without intention and purpose and plan.
So whenever you feel the plow's sharp blade
Let not your heart be sorely afraid,
For, like the farmer, God chooses a field
From which He expects an excellent yield.

LIGHT DIVINE

God is light; in him there is no darkness at all.

1 JOHN 1:5 NIV

I am Faith
    and I am Light,
And in Me
    there shall be no night.

Helen Steiner Rice

12
FEBRUARY

GLORIOUS PRAISE

Make a joyful noise to God, all the earth;
sing the glory of his name; give to him glorious praise!

PSALM 66:1–2 RSV

God's miracles
Are all around
Within our sight
And touch and sound.

One-Minute Meditations

13
FEBRUARY

SHIELD AGAINST DARKNESS

*This God—his way is perfect; the promise of
the LORD proves true; he is a shield for all
those who take refuge in him.*

PSALM 18:30 RSV

No day is too dark and no burden too great
For God in His love to penetrate
And know and believe
    without question or doubt
That no matter what happens
    God is there to help out.

Never Alone

He raises up the needy out of affliction.

Psalm 107:41 RSV

We never meet our problems alone,
For God is our Father and we are His own.
There's no circumstance we cannot meet
If we lay our burden at Jesus' feet.

KIND SPIRIT, GENTLE TONGUE

A gentle tongue is a tree of life,
but perverseness in it breaks the spirit.

PROVERBS 15:4 RSV

Like roses in a garden,
Kindness fills the air
With a certain bit of sweetness
As it touches everywhere.

Helen Steiner Rice

16

FEBRUARY

SOUL SUSTENANCE

The world and its desires pass away,
but the man who does the will of God lives forever.

1 JOHN 2:17 NIV

For though he reaches his earthly goal,
He'll waste away with a starving soul
But he who eats of the holy bread
Will always find his spirit fed,
And even the poorest of men can afford
To feast at the table prepared by the Lord.

Faith, Not Sight

You love him even though you have never seen him.
Though you do not see him now, you trust him;
and you rejoice with a glorious, inexpressible joy.

1 Peter 1:8 nlt

Though I cannot find Your hand
To lead me on to the promised land,
I still believe with all my being
Your hand is there beyond my seeing!

Helen Steiner Rice

18
FEBRUARY

INDISPENSABLE LOVE

*We have known and believed the love that God
hath to us. God is love; and he that dwelleth
in love dwelleth in God, and God in him.*

1 JOHN 4:16 KJV

Great is the power of might and mind,
But only love can make us kind,
And all we are or hope to be
Is empty pride and vanity.
If love is not a part of all,
The greatest man is very small.

BLESSINGS FOR MOURNERS

Blessed are they that mourn: for they shall be comforted.

MATTHEW 5:4 KJV

Through long hours of tribulation
God gives us time for meditation,
And no sickness can be counted loss
That teaches us to bear our cross.

Helen Steiner Rice

20 FEBRUARY

DEATH DEFUSED

*God is keeping careful watch over us and
the future. The Day is coming when you'll
have it all—life healed and whole.*

1 PETER 1:5 MSG

All who believe in the risen Lord
Have been assured of this reward,
And death for them is just graduation
To a higher realm of wide elevation.

UNSHAKABLE PEACE

*Peace I leave with you, my peace I give unto you:
not as the world giveth, give I unto you. Let not
your heart be troubled, neither let it be afraid.*

JOHN 14:27 KJV

When everything is quiet
    and we're lost in meditation,
Our souls are then preparing
    for a deeper dedication
That will make it wholly possible
    to quietly endure
The violent world around us,
    for in God we are secure.

HAVE PATIENCE

*Now the God of patience and consolation
grant you to be likeminded one toward
another according to Christ Jesus.*

ROMANS 15:5 KJV

God, teach me to be patient,
  teach me to go slow—
Teach me how to wait on You
  when my way I do not know.
Teach me to let go, dear God,
  and pray undisturbed until
My heart is filled with inner peace
  and I learn to know Your will.

23

FEBRUARY

EVERLASTING ALLY

Lo, I am with you alway,
even unto the end of the world.

MATTHEW 28:20 KJV

Remember me, God? I come every day
Just to talk with You, Lord,
   and to learn how to pray.
You make me feel welcome,
   You reach out Your hand.
I need never explain, for You understand.

Helen Steiner Rice

24
FEBRUARY

DOWN WITH PRIDE

*We break down every thought and proud thing that
puts itself up against the wisdom of God. We take
hold of every thought and make it obey Christ.*

2 CORINTHIANS 10:5 NLV

Take me and break me and make me,
    dear God, just what You want me to be.
Give me the strength to accept what You send
    and eyes with the vision to see
All the small, arrogant ways that I have
    and the vain little things that I do.
Make me aware that I'm often concerned
    more with myself than with You.

LIFE'S GARDEN

*"Lo, the winter is past, the rain is over and gone.
The flowers appear on the earth, the time of
singing has come, and the voice of the
turtledove is heard in our land."*

SONG OF SOLOMON 2:11–12 RSV

Life's lovely garden
Would be sweeter by far
If all who passed through it
Were as nice as you are.

26

FEBRUARY

JUST TRUST!

*We know that in all things God works for the good
of those who love him, who have been
called according to his purpose.*

ROMANS 8:28 NIV

Our Father in heaven
Always knows what is best,
And if you trust in His wisdom,
Your life will be blessed.

27
FEBRUARY

SECRET PRAYER

"Pray to your Father who is in secret;
and your Father who sees in secret will reward you."

MATTHEW 6:6 RSV

There's no need at all
For impressive prayer,
For the minute we seek God,
He is already there!

Helen Steiner Rice

28

FEBRUARY

SUSTAINING STRENGTH

*The Lord stood by me and gave me strength
to proclaim the message fully.*

2 TIMOTHY 4:17 RSV

When seen through God's eyes,
    earthly troubles diminish,
And we're given new strength
    to face and to finish,
Life's daily tasks as they come along,
If we but pray for strength to keep us strong.

SEEK AND FIND

The LORD is with you, while ye be with him;
and if ye seek him, he will be found of you.

2 CHRONICLES 15:2 KJV

God, help me in my feeble way
To somehow do something each day
To show You that I love You best
And that my faith will stand each test,
And let me serve You every day
And feel You near me when I pray.
Oh, hear my prayer, dear God above,
And make me worthy of Your love.

Helen Steiner Rice

1
MARCH

GOD OUR PROMISE KEEPER

We who have turned to [God] can have great comfort
knowing that He will do what He has promised.
This hope is a safe anchor for our souls. It will never
move. This hope goes into the Holiest Place of
All behind the curtain of heaven.

HEBREWS 6:18–19 NLV

So keep on believing
Whatever betides you,
Knowing that God will be
With you to guide you,
And all that He promised
Will be yours to receive
If you trust Him completely
And always believe.

2
MARCH

BORN ANEW

In hope of eternal life, which God, that cannot lie,
promised before the world began. . .

TITUS 1:2 KJV

The waking earth in springtime
Reminds us it is true
That nothing ever really dies
That is not born anew.

PRAY AND BELIEVE

*The effectual fervent prayer of a
righteous man availeth much.*

JAMES 5:16 KJV

Whenever I am troubled
    and lost in deep despair,
I bundle all my troubles up
    and go to God in prayer. . .
I know He stilled the tempest
    and calmed the angry sea,
And I humbly ask if, in His love,
    He'll do the same for me.

4
MARCH

PRAY WITH CONFIDENCE

*Know that the LORD hath set apart him that is godly
for himself: the LORD will hear when I call unto him.*

PSALM 4:3 KJV

Often we pause and wonder
     when we kneel down and pray
Can God really hear the prayers that we say?
But if we keep praying and talking to Him,
He'll brighten the soul
     that was clouded and dim.
And as we continue, our burden seems lighter;
Our sorrow is softened
     and our outlook is brighter.

5 MARCH

DAILY PRAYERS

O taste and see that the LORD is good!
Happy is the man who takes refuge in him!

PSALM 34:8 RSV

Brighten your day
And lighten your way;
Lessen your cares
With daily prayers.

PATIENCE PAYS OFF

I waited patiently for the LORD;
he inclined to me and heard my cry.

PSALM 40:1 RSV

Give us, through the coming year,
Quietness of mind;
Teach us to be patient
And always to be kind.

Helen Steiner Rice

7
MARCH

GRUMBLE NOT

Don't grumble against each other, brothers, or you will be judged. The Judge is standing at the door!

JAMES 5:9 NIV

Open up your hardened heart
And let God enter in—
He only wants to help you
A new life to begin.

LIGHT TO LEAD THE WAY

*"I have come as light into the world, that whoever
believes in me may not remain in darkness."*

JOHN 12:46 RSV

God, in Thy great wisdom,
Lead us in the way that's right,
And may the darkness of this world
Be conquered by Thy light.

Helen Steiner Rice

9
MARCH

HARVESTTIME

*He who supplies seed to the sower and bread for food
will also supply and increase your store of seed and
will enlarge the harvest of your righteousness.*

2 CORINTHIANS 9:10 NIV

Seed must be sown
To bring forth grain,
And nothing is born
Without suffering and pain.

BE GLAD

Be glad in the LORD, and rejoice, O righteous,
and shout for joy, all you upright in heart!

PSALM 32:11 RSV

Be glad that you've walked
   with courage for each day,
Be glad you've had strength
   for each step of the way,
Be glad for the comfort
   you've found in prayer,
But be gladdest of all for God's tender care.

Helen Steiner Rice

II
MARCH

HEED GOD'S VOICE

"Today, if you hear his voice, do not harden your hearts."

HEBREWS 3:7–8 NIV

Enjoy your sojourn on earth and be glad
That God gives you a choice
 between good things and bad,
And only be sure that you heed God's voice
Whenever life asks you to make a choice.

A MATTER OF PERSPECTIVE

*"You will seek me and find me when
you seek me with all your heart."*

JEREMIAH 29:13 NIV

When we view our problems
Through the eyes of God above,
Misfortunes turn to blessings,
And hatred turns to love.

Helen Steiner Rice

HOLY HARVEST

"While the earth remains, seedtime and harvest,
cold and heat, summer and winter,
day and night, shall not cease."

GENESIS 8:22 RSV

Rejoice though your heart
Is broken in two;
God seeks to bring forth
A rich harvest in you.

SHINE!

The light of the righteous shines brightly.

PROVERBS 13:9 NIV

When the darkness shuts out the light,
We must lean on faith to restore our sight,
For there is nothing we need to know
If we have faith that wherever we go
God will be there to help us bear
Our disappointments, pain, and care.

Helen Steiner Rice

15 MARCH

SECURE IN GOD'S LOVE

*I know that nothing can keep
us from the love of God.*

ROMANS 8:38 NLV

Just close your eyes and open your heart
And feel your cares and worries depart.
Just yield yourself to the Father above
And let Him hold you secure in His love.

16 MARCH

GOD OF MIRACLES

Call to remembrance the former days,
in which, after ye were illuminated,
ye endured a great fight of afflictions.

HEBREWS 10:32 KJV

Barren, windswept, lonely hills
Turning gold with daffodils—
These miracles are all around
Within our sight and touch and sound,
As true and wonderful today
As when the stone was rolled away,
Proclaiming to all doubting men
That in God all things live again.

Helen Steiner Rice

17
MARCH

GOD'S OWN

The Lord knoweth them that are his.

2 TIMOTHY 2:19 KJV

My cross is not too heavy,
    my road is not too rough
Because God walks beside me,
    and to know this is enough. . .
And though I get so lonely,
    I know I'm not alone,
For the Lord God is my Father
    and He loves me as His own.

POTENCY IN PRAYER

*Whatsoever ye shall ask in my name, that will I do,
that the Father may be glorified in the Son. If ye
shall ask any thing in my name, I will do it.*

JOHN 14:13–14 KJV

Prayer is much more than
    just asking for things—
It's the peace and contentment
    that quietness brings.
So thank You again
    for Your mercy and love
And for making me heir
    to Your kingdom above.

Helen Steiner Rice

19 MARCH

JESUS OUR CONSTANT COMPANION

This is the confidence that we have in him, that, if we ask any thing according to his will, he heareth us: and if we know that he hear us, whatsoever we ask, we know that we have the petitions that we desired of him.

1 JOHN 5:14–15 KJV

Somebody loves you more than you know,
Somebody goes with you wherever you go,
Somebody really and truly cares
And lovingly listens to all of your prayers.

TRUE HAPPINESS

"My spirit is happy in God."

LUKE 1:47 NLV

Trust in His wisdom and follow His ways
And be not concerned with
    the world's empty praise,
But first seek His kingdom
    and you will possess
The world's greatest of riches,
    which is true happiness.

Helen Steiner Rice

**21
MARCH**

MERCY AND LOVE

Blessed are the merciful: for they shall obtain mercy.

MATTHEW 5:7 KJV

"Love one another, as I have loved you"
May seem impossible to do,
But if you will try to trust and believe,
Great are the joys that you will receive.

22
MARCH

LIFE ETERNAL

"This is the will of my Father, that every one who sees the Son and believes in him should have eternal life; and I will raise him up at the last day."

JOHN 6:40 RSV

Our Savior's resurrection
Was God's way of telling men
That in Christ we are eternal
And in Him we live again.

Helen Steiner Rice

23 MARCH

ENDURING LOVE

*Thou, O LORD, art enthroned for ever;
thy name endures to all generations.*

PSALM 102:12 RSV

Kings and kingdoms all pass away;
Nothing on earth endures.
But the love of God, who sent His Son,
Is for ever and ever yours.

24
MARCH

DAILY GUEST

*May God be gracious to us and bless us
and make his face to shine upon us.*

PSALM 67:1 RSV

Every home is specially blessed
When God becomes a daily guest
For when two people pray together,
They also dream and stay together.

Helen Steiner Rice

25
MARCH

REMAIN IN LOVE

"As the Father has loved me, so have I loved you.
Now remain in my love. If you obey my commands,
you will remain in my love, just as I have obeyed
my Father's commands and remain in his love."

JOHN 15:9–10 NIV

Love works in ways that are
    wondrous and strange,
And there is nothing in life
    that love cannot change,
And all that God promised
    will someday come true
When you love one another
    the way He loved you.

26
MARCH

Take Faith Along

Love the LORD, all you his saints!
The LORD preserves the faithful, but abundantly
requites him who acts haughtily.

PSALM 31:23 RSV

As you climb life's ladder,
Take faith along with you,
And great will be your happiness
As your dearest dreams come true.

NEAR TO ME

*Honor the LORD with your substance and
with the first fruits of all your produce.*

PROVERBS 3:9 RSV

There is happiness in knowing
That my heart will always be
A place where I can hold You
And keep You near to me.

ETERNAL SPRING

"The hour is coming when all who are in the tombs will hear his voice and come forth."

JOHN 5:28–29 RSV

Man, like flowers, too, must sleep
Until he is called from the darkest deep
To live in that place where angels sing
And where there is eternal spring!

LOVE'S GENTLE LIGHT

For all the law is fulfilled in one word, even in this;
Thou shalt love thy neighbour as thyself.

GALATIANS 5:14 KJV

As soon as love entered the heart's open door,
The faults we once saw
   are not there anymore—
And the things that seem wrong
   begin to look right
When viewed in the softness
   of love's gentle light.

OUR FOREVER FRIEND

*Then shalt thou call, and the LORD shall answer;
thou shalt cry, and he shall say, Here I am.*

ISAIAH 58:9 KJV

How could I think God was far, far away
When I feel Him beside me
   every hour of the day?
And I've plenty of reasons
   to know God's my friend,
And this is one friendship
   that time cannot end.

Helen Steiner Rice

31
MARCH

EASE THE BURDEN

*For he that in these things serveth Christ is
acceptable to God, and approved of men. Let us
therefore follow after the things which make for peace,
and things wherewith one may edify another.*

ROMANS 14:18–19 KJV

If we would but forget our care
And stop in sympathy to share
The burden that our brother carried,
Our minds and hearts would be less harried
And we would feel our load was small—
In fact, we carried no load at all.

HEAVENLY STEPPING-STONES

Whatsoever things were written aforetime were written for our learning, that we through patience and comfort of the scriptures might have hope.

ROMANS 15:4 KJV

Life is a highway on which the years go by,
Sometimes the road is level,
 sometimes the hills are high. . .
But as we travel onward
 to a future that's unknown,
We can make each mile we travel
 a heavenly stepping-stone!

Helen Steiner Rice

2 APRIL

RADICAL KINDNESS

Love ye your enemies, and do good, and lend, hoping for nothing again; and your reward shall be great, and ye shall be the children of the Highest.

LUKE 6:35 KJV

It's not fortune or fame or worldwide acclaim
That makes for true greatness, you'll find—
It's the wonderful art of teaching the heart
To always be thoughtful and kind!

ONLY GOD

Though I walk in the midst of trouble, thou wilt revive me: thou shalt stretch forth thine hand against the wrath of mine enemies, and thy right hand shall save me.

PSALM 138:7 KJV

At times like these man is helpless. . .
It is only God
Who can speak the words
That calm the sea,
Still the wind,
And ease the pain. . .
So lean on Him
And you will never walk alone.

HE HAS RISEN!

They got up and returned at once to Jerusalem.
There they found the Eleven and those with them,
assembled together and saying, "It is true!
The Lord has risen and has appeared to Simon."

LUKE 24:33–34 NIV

He was crucified and buried,
But today the whole world knows
The Resurrection story
Of how Jesus Christ arose.

HAPPY MEMORIES

I thank my God every time I remember you.

PHILIPPIANS 1:3 NIV

Memories are treasures
Time cannot take away,
So may you be surrounded
By happy ones today.

Helen Steiner Rice

6
APRIL

Springtime

Be exalted, O God, above the heavens,
and let your glory be over all the earth.

PSALM 108:5 NIV

April comes with cheeks a-glowing,
Flowers bloom and streams are flowing,
And the earth in glad surprise
Opens wide its springtime eyes.

7
APRIL

HEAVEN-SENT

*He who gives heed to the word will prosper,
and happy is he who trusts in the LORD.*

PROVERBS 16:20 RSV

Happiness is giving up thoughts
That breed discontent
And accepting what comes
As a gift heaven-sent.

Helen Steiner Rice

8
APRIL

WIDER VISION

*"If you faithfully obey the commands I am giving you
today—to love the LORD your God and to serve him
with all your heart and with all your soul—then I will
send rain on your land in its season, both autumn
and spring rains, so that you may gather
in your grain, new wine and oil."*

DEUTERONOMY 11:13–14 NIV

God, give us wider vision
      to see and understand
That both the sun and showers
      are gifts from Thy great hand.

9 APRIL

Earth-Shaking Power

God has power over all things forever.

1 PETER 5:11 NLV

We have God's Easter promise,
    so let us seek a goal
That opens up new vistas
    for man's eternal soul. . .
For our strength and our security
    lie not in earthly things
But in Christ the Lord, who died for us
    and rose as King of kings.

Spring Thanksgiving

Give thanks to the LORD, for He is good!

Psalm 136:1 NKJV

April comes with cheeks a-glowing;
Silver streams are all a-flowing.
Flowers open wide their eyes
In lovely rapturous surprise.
Lilies dream beside the brooks,
Violets in meadow nooks,
And the birds gone wild with glee
Fill the woods with melody.

11
APRIL

GLAD HEART, HAPPY FACE

A glad heart makes a happy face.

PROVERBS 15:13 NLV

Cheerful thoughts like sunbeams
    lighten up the darkest fears,
For when the heart is happy
    there's just no time for tears,
And when the face is smiling
    it's impossible to frown,
And when you are high-spirited
    you cannot feel low-down.

ONLY BELIEVE

*If thou canst believe, all things
are possible to him that believeth.*

MARK 9:23 KJV

All we really ever need
Is faith as a grain of mustard seed,
For all God asks is, "Do you believe?"
For if you do, ye shall receive.

ALL-SURPASSING PEACE

*The peace of God, which passeth all understanding,
shall keep your hearts and minds through Christ Jesus.*

PHILIPPIANS 4:7 KJV

"Do not be anxious," said our Lord,
"Have peace from day to day—
The lilies neither toil nor spin,
Yet none are clothed as they."
The meadowlark with sweetest song
Fears not for bread or nest
Because he trusts our Father's love
And God knows what is best.

SPRINGTIME MIRACLES

*To us there is but one God, the Father, of whom are
all things, and we in him; and one Lord Jesus Christ,
by whom are all things, and we by him.*

1 CORINTHIANS 8:6 KJV

The sleeping earth awakens,
    the robins start to sing—
The flowers open wide their eyes
    to tell us it is spring.
These miracles of Easter,
    wrought with divine perfection,
Are the blessed reassurance
    of our Savior's resurrection.

15 APRIL

GOD'S WILL, NOT OURS

*Whatsoever we ask, we receive of him,
because we keep his commandments, and do
those things that are pleasing in his sight.*

1 JOHN 3:22 KJV

There can be no crown of stars
Without a cross to bear,
And there is no salvation
Without faith and love and prayer.
And when we take our needs to God,
Let us pray as did His Son
That dark night in Gethsemane—
"Thy will, not mine, be done."

Helen Steiner Rice

16
APRIL

THE ROAD
CALLED REMEMBRANCE

Think of other people as more important than yourself.

PHILIPPIANS 2:3 NLV

Memory builds a little pathway
    that goes winding through my heart.
It's a lovely, quiet, gentle trail
    from other things apart.
I only meet when traveling there
    the folks I like the best,
For this road I call remembrance
    is hidden from the rest.

17
APRIL

TRUST HIM

Blessed is that man that maketh the LORD
his trust, and respecteth not the proud,
nor such as turn aside to lies.

PSALM 40:4 KJV

God, in His wisdom and mercy, looked down
    on His children below
And gave them the privilege of choosing
    the right or the wrong way to go. . .
So trust in His almighty wisdom
    and enjoy the fruit of His love,
And life on earth will be happy
    as you walk with the Father above.

Helen Steiner Rice

18 APRIL

BRAND-NEW START

*He who looks into the perfect law, the law of liberty,
and perseveres, being no hearer that forgets but a
doer that acts, he shall be blessed in his doing.*

JAMES 1:25 RSV

It does not take a special time
To make a brand-new start;
It only takes the deep desire
To try with all your heart.

GET UNDERSTANDING

To get wisdom is better than gold;
to get understanding is to be chosen rather than silver.

PROVERBS 16:16 RSV

To understand God's greatness
And to use His gifts each day,
The soul must learn to meet Him
In a meditative way.

MARVELOUS MIGHT

*O sing to the LORD a new song, for he has
done marvelous things! His right hand and
his holy arm have gotten him victory.*

PSALM 98:1 RSV

God's mighty hand
Can be felt every minute,
For there is nothing on earth
That God isn't in it.

SMALL DEEDS, BIG RESULTS

He stores up sound wisdom for the upright;
he is a shield to those who walk in integrity, guarding
the paths of justice and preserving the way of his saints.

PROVERBS 2:7–8 RSV

Seldom do we realize
The importance of small deeds
Or to what degree of greatness
Unnoticed kindness leads.

Helen Steiner Rice

22
APRIL

NEW HOPE

The hope of the righteous will be gladness.

PROVERBS 10:28 NKJV

No matter how downhearted
　　and discouraged we may be,
New hope is born when we behold
　　leaves budding on a tree,
And troubles seem to vanish
　　when robins start to sing,
For God never sends the winter
　　without the joy of spring.

23
APRIL

PUT YOUR PAST BEHIND

"Forget the former things;
do not dwell on the past."

ISAIAH 43:18 NIV

No matter what your past has been,
Trust God to understand,
And no matter what your problem is,
Just place it in His hand.

Helen Steiner Rice

GENTLY HUMBLE

*[Jesus] said to the woman,
"Your faith has saved you; go in peace."*

LUKE 7:50 RSV

Keep us gently humble
In the greatness of Thy love,
So someday we are fit to dwell
With Thee in peace above.

LOVE OVERLOOKS OFFENSES

Love must be sincere.

ROMANS 12:9 NIV

Love makes us patient,
    understanding, and kind,
And we judge with our hearts
    and not with our minds,
For as soon as love enters
    the heart's open door,
The faults we once saw
    are not there anymore.

Enfolded in God's Love

"If you abide in me, and my words abide in you,
ask whatever you will, and it shall be done for you."

John 15:7 rsv

I said a little prayer for you,
And I asked the Lord above
To keep you safely in His care
And enfold you in His love.

27
APRIL

SWEET BLESSINGS

"I will send down showers in season;
there will be showers of blessing."

EZEKIEL 34:26 NIV

Wishing God's sweet blessings
Not in droplets but a shower,
To fall on you throughout the day
And brighten every hour.

Helen Steiner Rice

28
APRIL

HEAR MY PLEA, LORD

Give heed to me, O LORD, and hearken to my plea.

JEREMIAH 18:19 RSV

Lord, I'm unworthy, I know,
   but I do love You so—
I beg You to answer my plea.
I've not much to give, but as long as I live,
May I give it completely to Thee!

29 APRIL

SAFE IN GOD'S CARE

*I long to dwell in your tent forever and
take refuge in the shelter of your wings.*

PSALM 61:4 NIV

All who have God's blessing
Can rest safely in His care,
For He promises safe passage
On the wings of faith and prayer.

Helen Steiner Rice

30
APRIL

SHELTER OF LOVE

The Lord takes care of all who love Him.

PSALM 145:20 NLV

God's love is like an island
    in life's ocean vast and wide—
A peaceful, quiet shelter
    from the restless, rising tide.
God's love is like a fortress,
    and we seek protection there
When the waves of tribulation
    seem to drown us in despair.

TRIUMPHANT JOY

Ye now therefore have sorrow:
but I will see you again, and your heart shall rejoice,
and your joy no man taketh from you.

JOHN 16:22 KJV

Wish not for the easy way
    to win your heart's desire,
For the joy's in overcoming
    and withstanding flood and fire,
For to triumph over trouble
    and grow stronger with defeat
Is to win the kind of victory
    that will make your life complete.

A Union of Love

Ye yourselves are taught of God to love one another.

1 Thessalonians 4:9 KJV

When you walk with God each day
And kneel together when you pray,
Your marriage will be truly blessed
And God will be your daily guest,
And love that once seemed yours alone
God gently blends into His own.

3 MAY

EMBRACE MERCY

Be ye therefore merciful, as your Father also is merciful.

LUKE 6:36 KJV

Open up your hardened hearts
    and let God enter in,
He only wants to help you a new life to begin,
And every day's a good day
    to lose yourself in others,
And anytime's a good time
    to see mankind as brothers,
And this can only happen
    when you realize it's true
That everyone needs someone
    and that someone is you.

Helen Steiner Rice

4
MAY

GLIMPSE OF HEAVEN

*Now the God of hope fill you with all joy and
peace in believing, that ye may abound in hope,
through the power of the Holy Ghost.*

ROMANS 15:13 KJV

Once again I've met You, God,
And worshipped on Your holy sod. . .
For who could see the dawn break through
Without a glimpse of heaven and You?

Don't Despise Discipline

*Blessed is the man you discipline, O LORD,
the man you teach from your law.*

PSALM 94:12 NIV

When we fail to heed His voice,
We leave the Lord no other choice
Except to use a firm, stern hand
To make us know He's in command.

TRUST IN GOD'S LOVE

*I trust in the steadfast love of
God for ever and ever.*

PSALM 52:8 RSV

Whatever our problems,
Our troubles and sorrows,
If we trust in the Lord,
There'll be brighter tomorrows.

7 MAY

WHATEVER IS BEST

How great is the love the Father has lavished on us,
that we should be called children of God!
And that is what we are!

1 JOHN 3:1 NIV

Whatever we ask for
    falls short of God's giving,
For His greatness exceeds every facet of living,
And always God's ready and eager and willing
To pour out His mercy, completely fulfilling
All of man's needs for peace, joy, and rest,
For God gives His children whatever is best.

Helen Steiner Rice

8
MAY

WARM WELCOME

Welcome one another, therefore,
as Christ has welcomed you, for the glory of God.

ROMANS 15:7 RSV

You make me feel welcome,
You reach out Your hand;
I need never explain,
For You understand.

9
MAY

GOD OUR PROBLEM SOLVER

A wise man listens to advice.

PROVERBS 12:15 RSV

We all have cares and problems
We cannot solve alone,
But if we go to God in prayer,
We are never on our own.

Helen Steiner Rice

10
MAY

NEW AWARENESS

One man pretends to be rich, yet has nothing;
another pretends to be poor, yet has great wealth.

PROVERBS 13:7 RSV

Thank You, God, for the miracles
We are much too blind to see;
Give us new awareness
Of our many gifts from Thee.

WORDS TO LIVE BY

*"The Spirit alone gives eternal life. Human
effort accomplishes nothing. And the very words
I have spoken to you are spirit and life."*

JOHN 6:63 NLT

We all need words to live by,
To inspire us and guide us,
Words to give us courage
When the trials of life betide us.
And the words that never fail us
Are the words of God above,
Words of comfort and of courage
Filled with wisdom and with love.

Helen Steiner Rice

EMPTY TOMB, AWESOME GOD

They were on their way to the tomb and they asked each other, "Who will roll the stone away from the entrance of the tomb?" But when they looked up, they saw that the stone, which was very large, had been rolled away.

MARK 16:2–4 NIV

Miracles are all around
Within our sight and touch and sound,
As true and wonderful today
As when the stone was rolled away.

13 MAY

FOREVER ON MY MIND

Finally, be ye all of one mind,
having compassion one of another, love as brethren,
be pitiful, be courteous.

1 PETER 3:8 KJV

You cannot go beyond my thoughts
  or leave my love behind
Because I keep you in my heart
  and forever on my mind. . .
And though I may not tell you,
  I think you know it's true
That I find daily happiness
  in the very thought of you.

Helen Steiner Rice

14
MAY

FOOTSTEPS OF LOVE

A new commandment I give unto you, that ye love one another; as I have loved you, that ye also love one another. By this shall all men know that ye are my disciples, if ye have love one to another.

JOHN 13:34–35 KJV

Love changes darkness into light
And makes the heart take wingless flight.
Oh, blessed are those who walk in love—
They also walk with God above.

15 MAY

MORE LIKE CHRIST

You are being made more like Christ.
He is the One Who made you.

COLOSSIANS 3:10 NLV

May you find rich satisfaction
In your daily work and prayer,
And in knowing as you serve Him
He will keep you in His care.

Helen Steiner Rice

16
MAY

CHILDLIKE FAITH

*Let us draw near with a true heart in full assurance of
faith, having our hearts sprinkled from an evil conscience,
and our bodies washed with pure water.*

HEBREWS 10:22 KJV

Only a child can completely accept
What probing adults research and reject.
O Father, grant once more to men
A simple, childlike faith again,
For only by faith and faith alone
Can we approach our Father's throne.

LIGHTEN THE LOAD

Blessed be the Lord, who daily bears us up;
God is our salvation.

PSALM 68:19 RSV

Each day as it comes
    brings a chance to each one
To live to the fullest, leaving nothing undone
That would brighten the life
    or lighten the load
Of some weary traveler lost on life's road.

Helen Steiner Rice

18 MAY

HOLD ON TO HOPE

*Why are you cast down, O my soul, and why are
you disquieted within me? Hope in God; for I
shall again praise him, my help and my God.*

PSALM 43:5 RSV

God enters the heart
    that is broken with sorrow
As He opens the door to a brighter tomorrow,
For only through tears can we recognize
The suffering that lies in another's eyes.

Heart Song

The LORD is my strength and my shield; in him my heart trusts; so I am helped, and my heart exults, and with my song I give thanks to him.

PSALM 28:7 RSV

Thank You again
For Your mercy and love
And for making me heir
To Your kingdom above!

GOD AT MY SIDE

*"When you pass through the waters I will be with you;
and through the rivers, they shall not overwhelm you;
when you walk through fire you shall not be burned,
and the flame shall not consume you."*

ISAIAH 43:2 RSV

My cross is not too heavy,
My road is not too rough,
Because God walks beside me,
And to know this is enough.

LOVE'S BLESSING

"I have loved you with an everlasting love."

JEREMIAH 31:3 NIV

Love is the language that
    every heart speaks,
For love is the one thing
    that every heart seeks. . .
And where there is love
    God, too, will abide
And bless the family residing inside.

Helen Steiner Rice

LOVE BEYOND DESCRIPTION

*In this was manifested the love of God toward us,
because that God sent his only begotten Son into
the world, that we might live through him.*

1 JOHN 4:9 KJV

What is love? No words can define it—
It's something so great
    only God could design it.
Wonder of wonders,
    beyond man's conception—
And only in God can love find true perfection.

23
MAY

MARVELOUS WORKS

I will praise thee, O LORD, with my whole heart;
I will shew forth all thy marvellous works.

PSALM 9:1 KJV

I come to meet You, God, and as I linger here
I seem to feel You very near.
A rustling leaf, a rolling slope
Speak to my heart of endless hope.
The sun just rising in the sky,
The waking birdlings as they fly,
The grass all wet with morning dew
Are telling me I just met You.

OUR FAITHFUL GOD

*Know therefore that the LORD thy God, he is God,
the faithful God, which keepeth covenant and
mercy with them that love him and keep his
commandments to a thousand generations.*

DEUTERONOMY 7:9 KJV

Sometimes when faith is running low
And I cannot fathom why things are so,
I walk among the flowers that grow
And learn the answers to all I would know. . .
For among my flowers I have come to see
Life's miracle and its mystery,
And standing in silence and reverie,
My faith comes flooding back to me.

**25
MAY**

BUILD 'EM UP

*Each of us should please his neighbor
for his good, to build him up.*

ROMANS 15:2 NIV

God lives in the beauty
    that comes with spring—
The colorful flower, the birds that sing—
And He lives in people as kind as you,
And He lives in all the nice things you do.

Helen Steiner Rice

EVERLASTING LOVE

"I have loved you with an everlasting love;
I have drawn you with loving-kindness."

JEREMIAH 31:3 NIV

Nothing on earth or in heaven can part
A love that has grown to be part of the heart
And just like the sun and the stars and the sea,
This love will go on through eternity,
For true love lives on when earthly things die,
For it's part of the spirit that soars to the sky.

27 MAY

CHERISHED FRIENDS

A man that hath friends must shew himself friendly:
and there is a friend that sticketh closer than a brother.

PROVERBS 18:24 KJV

Life is a garden, good friends are the flowers,
And times spent together
   are life's happiest hours. . .
And friendship, like flowers,
   blooms ever more fair
When carefully tended
   by dear friends who care.

LOVE WITHOUT END

Love never comes to an end.

1 CORINTHIANS 13:8 NLV

Love is like magic and it always will be,
For love still remains life's sweet mystery.
Love works in ways
    that are wondrous and strange,
And there's nothing in life
    that love cannot change.

NO BURDEN TOO GREAT FOR GOD

Be not wise in your own eyes;
fear the LORD, and turn away from evil.

PROVERBS 3:7 RSV

What more can we ask of our Father
Than to know we are never alone,
That His mercy and love are unfailing,
And He makes all our problems His own.

30 MAY

GREAT IN GOD'S EYES

Thou art my hope in the day of evil.

JEREMIAH 17:17 KJV

Let me say no to the flattery and praise
And quietly spend the rest of my days
Far from the greed and the speed of man,
Who has so distorted God's simple life plan,
And let me be great in the eyes of You, Lord,
For that is the richest, most priceless reward.

TRUST AND BELIEVE

The wise of heart will heed commandments.

PROVERBS 10:8 RSV

You need nothing more
    than God's guidance and love
To ensure the things
    that you're most worthy of. . .
So trust in His wisdom and follow His ways
And be not concerned
    with the world's empty praise,
But first seek His kingdom,
    and you will possess
The world's greatest riches,
    which is true happiness.

Helen Steiner Rice

OUR KEEPER

*The LORD is your keeper; the LORD is your
shade on your right hand. The sun shall not
smite you by day, nor the moon by night.*

PSALM 121:5–6 RSV

After the night, the morning,
Bidding all darkness cease;
After life's cares and sorrows,
The comfort and sweetness of peace.

**2
JUNE**

RICH BLESSINGS

*The blessing of the LORD makes rich,
and he adds no sorrow with it.*

PROVERBS 10:22 RSV

Be glad for the comfort
You've found in prayer;
Be glad for God's blessings,
His love and His care.

Helen Steiner Rice

3
JUNE

WHOLEHEARTED LOVE

We love, because he first loved us.

I JOHN 4:19 RSV

All of God's treasures
Are yours to share
If you love Him completely
And show Him you care.

GROW THAT FRUIT!

*The fruit of the Spirit is love, joy, peace,
longsuffering, gentleness, goodness, faith, meekness,
temperance: against such there is no law.*

GALATIANS 5:22–23 KJV

The more we endure with patience and grace,
The stronger we grow
    and the more we can face—
And the more we can face, the greater our love,
And with love in our hearts
    we are more conscious of
The pain and the sorrow in lives everywhere—
So it is through trouble that we learn to share.

Helen Steiner Rice

5
JUNE

BRILLIANT HOPE

*I pray also that the eyes of your heart may be enlightened
in order that you may know the hope to which
he has called you, the riches of his glorious
inheritance in the saints.*

EPHESIANS 1:18 NIV

In sickness or health,
In suffering and pain,
In storm-laden skies,
In sunshine and rain,
God always is there
To lighten your way
And lead you through darkness
To a much brighter day.

6
JUNE

TEARS TO SMILES

"[God] will wipe every tear from their eyes.
There will be no more death or mourning or crying
or pain, for the old order of things has passed away."

REVELATION 21:4 NIV

In God is our encouragement
In trouble and in trials,
And in suffering and in sorrow
He will turn our tears to smiles.

GODLY TRAINING

Train up a child in the way he should go,
and when he is old he will not depart from it.

PROVERBS 22:6 RSV

We are all God's children,
And He loves us, every one,
And freely and completely
Forgives all that we have done.

8
JUNE

No Time Like the Present

Behold, now is the acceptable time;
behold, now is the day of salvation.

2 Corinthians 6:2 RSV

How will you use the days of this year
And the time God has placed in your hands—
Will you waste the minutes
    and squander the hours,
Leaving no prints behind in time's sand?

Helen Steiner Rice

9
JUNE

Praise Him Day by Day

Every day I will bless thee,
and praise thy name for ever and ever.
Great is the LORD, and greatly to be praised,
and his greatness is unsearchable.

PSALM 145:2–3 RSV

Start every day
With a "good morning" prayer,
And God will bless each thing you do
And keep you in His care.

HEART HELP

*Keep your heart with all vigilance;
for from it flow the springs of life.*

PROVERBS 4:23 RSV

God's kindness is ever around you,
Always ready to freely impart
Strength to your faltering spirit,
Cheer to your lonely heart.

LIGHT BRIGHT

*Light dawns for the righteous,
and joy for the upright in heart.*

PSALM 97:II RSV

You can't light a candle
To show others the way
Without feeling the warmth
Of that bright little ray.

To God Be the Glory

I have looked upon thee in the sanctuary,
beholding thy power and glory.

Psalm 63:2 RSV

Show me the way, not to fortune or fame,
Not to win laurels or praise for my name,
But show me the way to spread the great story
That Thine is the kingdom
       and power and glory.

ABUNDANT MERCY

Answer me, O LORD, for thy steadfast love is good;
according to thy abundant mercy, turn to me.

PSALM 69:16 RSV

God in His mercy looks down on us all,
And though what we've done
   is so pitifully small,
He makes us feel welcome
   to kneel down and pray
For the chance to do better
   as we start a new day.

14
JUNE

THE TREASURE OF FRIENDSHIP

A friend loves at all times.

PROVERBS 17:17 RSV

Friendship is a golden chain;
The links are friends so dear,
And like a rare and precious jewel,
It's treasured more each year.

Helen Steiner Rice

**15
JUNE**

Our Prayers, God's Delight

*The sacrifice of the wicked is an abomination to
the LORD, but the prayer of the upright is his delight.*

PROVERBS 15:8 RSV

Games can't be won
Unless they are played,
And prayers can't be answered
Unless they are prayed.

MORNING THANKS

*Praise the LORD! O give thanks to the LORD,
for he is good; for his steadfast love endures for ever!*

PSALM 106:1 RSV

No day is unmeetable
If on rising, our first thought
Is to thank God for the blessings
That His loving care has brought.

Helen Steiner Rice

NIGHT AND DAY

Thine is the day, thine also the night;
thou hast established the luminaries and the sun.

PSALM 74:16 RSV

Who but God
     could make the day
And softly put
     the night away?

HAPPY HEART

"My heart is happy in the Lord."

1 SAMUEL 2:1 NLV

A wish that's sent with lots of love
Just seems to have a feeling—
A special word of sentiment
That makes it more appealing.
And that's the kind of loving wish
That's being sent your way
To hope that every day will be
Your happy kind of day.

Helen Steiner Rice

19 JUNE

HE HEARS MY VOICE

Evening, and morning, and at noon, will I pray,
and cry aloud: and he shall hear my voice.

PSALM 55:17 KJV

Spare me no heartache or sorrow, dear Lord,
For the heart that hurts
    reaps the richest reward,
And God blesses the heart
    that is broken with sorrow
As He opens the door to a brighter tomorrow.

One-Minute Meditations

20 JUNE

DON'T LOSE FAITH

"Be strong and have strength of heart!
Do not be afraid or lose faith. For the Lord
your God is with you anywhere you go."

JOSHUA 1:9 NLV

There's truly nothing we need know
If we have that faith wherever we go
God will be there to help us bear
Our disappointments, pain, and care.
For He is our Shepherd,
    our Father, our Guide,
And we're never alone
    with the Lord at our side.

Helen Steiner Rice

SERVE OTHERS, PLEASE GOD

God has chosen you. You are holy and loved by Him.
Because of this, your new life should be full of loving-pity.
You should be kind to others and have no pride.
Be gentle and be willing to wait for others.

COLOSSIANS 3:12 NLV

When we bring some pleasure
    to another human heart,
We have followed in His footsteps
    and we've had a little part
In serving God who loves us—
    for I'm very sure it's true
That in serving those around us,
    we serve and please God, too.

CHANNEL OF BLESSING

*He that hath my commandments, and keepeth them,
he it is that loveth me: and he that loveth me shall
be loved of my Father, and I will love him,
and will manifest myself to him.*

JOHN 14:21 KJV

Make me a channel of blessing today—
I ask again and again when I pray.
Do I turn a deaf ear to the Master's voice
Or refuse to hear His direction and choice?
I only know at the end of the day
That I did so little to pay my way.

FAITHFUL FRIEND

For thou, Lord, art good, and ready to forgive;
and plenteous in mercy unto all them that call upon thee.

PSALM 86:5 KJV

Somebody cares and always will—
The world forgets, but God loves you still
You cannot go beyond His love
No matter what you're guilty of,
For God forgives until the end—
He is your faithful, loyal friend.

24
JUNE

WORTHY OF HIS LOVE

*Fear ye not therefore, ye are of
more value than many sparrows.*

MATTHEW 10:31 KJV

When you're overwhelmed with fears
And all your hopes are drenched in tears,
Think not that life has been unfair
And given you too much to bear,
For God has chosen you because,
With all your weaknesses and flaws,
He feels that you are worthy of
The greatness of His wondrous love.

REDEEM THE TIME

*He came to the disciples and found them sleeping;
and he said to Peter, "So, could you
not watch with me one hour?"*

MATTHEW 26:40 RSV

God, grant us grace to use
　　all the hours of our days
Not for our selfish interests
　　and our own willful ways.

GOD'S ABIDING PRESENCE

*Thou dost show me the path of life;
in thy presence there is fulness of joy, in thy
right hand are pleasures for evermore.*

PSALM 16:11 RSV

God's presence is ever beside you,
As near as the reach of your hand;
You have but to tell Him your troubles—
There is nothing He won't understand.

Helen Steiner Rice

27
JUNE

Trust God's Timing

*[Jesus] told them, "You don't get to know
the time. Timing is the Father's business.
What you'll get is the Holy Spirit."*

ACTS 1:7 MSG

Never dread tomorrow
   or what the future brings
Just pray for strength and courage
   and trust God in all things,
And never grow discouraged—
   be patient and just wait,
For God never comes too early,
   and He never comes too late.

28

JUNE

OUR BURDEN-BEARER

*When the cares of my heart are many,
thy consolations cheer my soul.*

PSALM 94:19 RSV

Let me stop complaining
About my load of care,
For God will always lighten it
When it gets too much to bear.

CHEERFUL GIVERS

*Every man according as he purposeth in his heart,
so let him give; not grudgingly, or of necessity:
for God loveth a cheerful giver.*

2 CORINTHIANS 9:7 KJV

It's a wonderful world, and it's people like you
Who make it that way
   by the things that they do.
For a warm, ready smile
   or a kind, thoughtful deed
Or a hand outstretched in an hour of need
Can change our whole outlook
   and make the world bright.

BOOMERANG BLESSINGS

Give, and it shall be given unto you;
good measure, pressed down, and shaken together,
and running over, shall men give into your bosom.
For with the same measure that ye mete withal
it shall be measured to you again.

LUKE 6:38 KJV

If everybody brightened up the spot
    on which they're standing
By being more considerate
    and a little less demanding,
This dark old world would very soon
    eclipse the evening star—
If everybody brightened up the corner
    where they are!

Helen Steiner Rice

I
JULY

BLESSED TO BE A BLESSING

*Being enriched in every thing to all bountifulness,
which causeth through us thanksgiving to God.*

2 CORINTHIANS 9:11 KJV

In this troubled world it's refreshing to find
Someone who still has the time to be kind,
Someone who still has the faith to believe
That the more that you give,
    the more you receive,
Someone who's ready by thought,
    word, or deed
To reach out a hand in the hour of need.

**2
JULY**

WHEN TROUBLED,
TRUST!

*We are troubled on every side, yet not distressed;
we are perplexed, but not in despair; persecuted,
but not forsaken; cast down, but not destroyed.*

2 CORINTHIANS 4:8–9 KJV

You are so great. . .we are so small. . .
And when trouble comes, as it does to us all,
There's so little we can do
Except to place our trust in You.

Helen Steiner Rice

3
JULY

Thankful Hearts

*Let the peace of Christ have power over your
hearts. You were chosen as a part of
His body. Always be thankful.*

<small>Colossians 3:15 nlv</small>

Everyone needs someone to be thankful for,
And each day of life we are aware of this more,
For the joy of enjoying
    and the fullness of living
Are found only in hearts
    that are filled with thanksgiving.

HINTS OF GLORY

*Rooted and built up in him, and stablished
in the faith, as ye have been taught,
abounding therein with thanksgiving.*

COLOSSIANS 2:7 KJV

My garden beautifies my yard
   and adds fragrance to the air,
But it is also my cathedral
   and my quiet place of prayer.
So little do we realize that
   the glory and the power
Of Him who made the universe
   lie hidden in a flower!

Helen Steiner Rice

5
JULY

PRACTICE KINDNESS

He that giveth, let him do it with simplicity;
he that ruleth, with diligence; he that
sheweth mercy, with cheerfulness.

ROMANS 12:8 KJV

Kindness is a virtue given by the Lord—
It pays dividends in happiness
    and joy is its reward.
For if you practice kindness
    in all you say and do,
The Lord will wrap His kindness
    around your heart and you.

6
JULY

LOVE'S BEACON

*Hope maketh not ashamed; because the love of
God is shed abroad in our hearts by the
Holy Ghost which is given unto us.*

ROMANS 5:5 KJV

Open your heart's door and let Christ come in,
And He'll give you new life
and free you from sin—
And there is no joy that can ever compare
With the joy of knowing you're in God's care.

Helen Steiner Rice

7
JULY

UNSEEING EYE

*As it is written, Eye hath not seen, nor ear heard,
neither have entered into the heart of man, the things
which God hath prepared for them that love him.*

1 CORINTHIANS 2:9 KJV

Give me perception to make me aware
That scattered profusely on life's thoroughfare
Are the best gifts of God that we daily pass by
As we look at the world with an unseeing eye.

GOD'S GOOD EARTH

*For every creature of God is good, and nothing to
be refused, if it be received with thanksgiving.*

1 TIMOTHY 4:4 KJV

God's mighty hand can be felt everywhere,
For there's nothing on earth
    that is not in God's care.
The sky and the stars, the waves and the sea,
The dew on the grass, the leaves on a tree
Are constant reminders of God
    and His nearness
Proclaiming His presence with
    crystal-like clearness.

Helen Steiner Rice

9
JULY

FOLLOW THE SAVIOR

God looks down from heaven upon the sons of men to see if there are any that are wise, that seek after God.

PSALM 53:2 RSV

"Take up your cross and follow Me,"
The Savior said to man;
"Trust always in the greatness
Of My Father's holy plan."

10 JULY

UNTOLD BLESSINGS

Happy the people to whom such blessings fall!
Happy the people whose God is the LORD!

PSALM 144:15 RSV

Happiness is waking up
And beginning the day
By counting our blessings
And kneeling to pray.

Helen Steiner Rice

11
JULY

HIS TENDER TOUCH

*The sun shall not smite you by day,
nor the moon by night.*

PSALM 121:6 RSV

I see the dew glisten in crystal-like splendor
While God, with a touch
    that is gentle and tender,
Wraps up the night and softly tucks it away
And hangs out the sun to herald a new day.

No Worries

*"Therefore I tell you,
do not be anxious about your life."*

MATTHEW 6:25 RSV

When our lives are overcast
With trouble and with care,
Give us faith to see beyond
The dark clouds of despair.

Helen Steiner Rice

13
JULY

GOD OUR STRONGHOLD

The LORD is a stronghold to him
whose way is upright.

PROVERBS 10:29 RSV

There are many things in life
We cannot understand,
But we must trust God's judgment
And be guided by His hand.

14
JULY

SERENE IN OUR FATHER'S LOVE

*"Whatever you ask in prayer,
you will receive, if you have faith."*

MATTHEW 21:22 RSV

May I stand undaunted, come what may,
Secure in the knowledge I have only to pray
And ask my Creator and Father above
To keep me serene in His grace and His love!

Helen Steiner Rice

15
JULY

EYES THAT SEE

*Turning to the disciples he said privately,
"Blessed are the eyes which see what you see! For I
tell you that many prophets and kings desired
to see what you see, and did not see it."*

LUKE 10:23–24 RSV

Widen the vision of my unseeing eyes,
So in passing faces I'll recognize
Not just a stranger, unloved and unknown,
But a friend with a heart
    that is much like my own.

GOD'S BATTLE

"The battle is not yours, but God's."

2 CHRONICLES 20:15 NIV

Thank God for good things
He has already done,
And be grateful to Him
For the battles you've won.

Helen Steiner Rice

STUCK ON YOU

Do not leave your own friend. . .alone.

PROVERBS 27:10 NLV

I'd like to be a raindrop
Just falling on your hand,
I'd like to be a blade of grass
On which your dear feet stand,
I'd like to be your shadow
As it moves around all day,
I'd like to be most anything
That hangs around your way.

BRIMMING WITH THANKSGIVING

*Unto thee, O God, do we give thanks, unto
thee do we give thanks: for that thy name
is near thy wondrous works declare.*

PSALM 75:1 KJV

Thank You, God, for little things
    that come unexpectedly
To brighten up a dreary day
    that dawned so dismally.
Thank You, God, for brushing
    the dark clouds from my mind
And leaving only sunshine
    and joy of heart behind.

Helen Steiner Rice

19 JULY

SAVED TO SERVE

*Thou hast turned for me my mourning
into dancing: thou hast put off my sackcloth,
and girded me with gladness.*

PSALM 30:11 KJV

Father, I have knowledge,
    so will You show me now
How to use it wisely
    and to find a way somehow
To make the world I live in a little better place
And to make life with its problems
    a bit easier to face?
Grant me faith and courage,
    and put purpose in my days,
And show me how to serve Thee
    in the most effective ways.

FAITH FOR THE JOURNEY

*Come unto me, all ye that labour and are
heavy laden, and I will give you rest.*

MATTHEW 11:28 KJV

Faith to believe when the way is rough
And faith to hang on when the going is tough
Will never fail to pull us through
And bring us strength and comfort, too.

Helen Steiner Rice

21
JULY

THE GIFT OF FRIENDSHIP

For if they fall, the one will lift up his fellow:
but woe to him that is alone when he falleth;
for he hath not another to help him up.

ECCLESIASTES 4:10 KJV

Friendship is a priceless gift
    that cannot be bought or sold
But its value is far greater
    than a mountain made of gold.

He Knows Our Needs

*Your Father knoweth what things ye
have need of, before ye ask him.*

MATTHEW 6:8 KJV

Hear me, blessed Jesus,
   as I say my prayers today,
And tell me You are close to me
   and You'll never go away. . .
And tell me that You love me
   like the Bible says You do,
And tell me also, Jesus,
   I can always come to You.

Helen Steiner Rice

23
JULY

NO STRANGERS

*"Then the King will say to those at his right hand, 'Come,
O blessed of my Father, inherit the kingdom prepared for
you from the foundation of the world; for I was hungry
and you gave me food, I was thirsty and you gave me
drink, I was a stranger and you welcomed me.' "*

MATTHEW 25:34–35 RSV

No one is a stranger in God's sight,
For God is love, and in His light
May we, too, try in our small way
To make new friends from day to day.

No Room for Blessings

"Do not worry about tomorrow,
for tomorrow will worry about itself.
Each day has enough trouble of its own."

MATTHEW 6:34 NIV

Refuse to be discouraged—
   refuse to be distressed,
For when we are despondent,
   our lives cannot be blessed.
Doubt and fear and worry
   close the door to faith and prayer,
And there's no room for blessings
   when we're lost in deep despair.

UNCHANGING LOVE

As for me, my prayer is to thee, O LORD.
At an acceptable time, O God, in the abundance
of thy steadfast love answer me.

PSALM 69:13 RSV

In this changing world,
May God's unchanging love
Surround and bless you daily
In abundance from above.

SIMPLE FAITH

We walk by faith, not by sight.

2 CORINTHIANS 5:7 ESV

Faith in things we cannot see
Requires a child's simplicity—
Oh Father, grant once more
    to women and men
A simple, childlike faith again.

Helen Steiner Rice

Be Content

There is great gain in godliness with contentment;
for we brought nothing into the world,
and we cannot take anything out of the world.

1 Timothy 6:6–7 RSV

Happiness is giving up wishing
   for things we have not
And making the best of whatever we've got—
It's knowing that life is determined for us
And pursuing our tasks
   without fret, fume, or fuss.

FAITH ON TRIAL

I kept my faith, even when I said,
"I am greatly afflicted."

PSALM 116:10 RSV

God, help me in my own small way
To somehow do something each day
To show You that I love You best
And that my faith will stand each test.

MERCIFUL DISCIPLINE

The Lord disciplines those he loves.

HEBREWS 12:6 NIV

Let us face the trouble
That is ours this present minute
And count on God to help us
And to put His mercy in it.

BE A BURDEN-BEARER

*Bear ye one another's burdens,
and so fulfil the law of Christ.*

GALATIANS 6:2 KJV

So many things in the line of duty
Drain us of effort and leave us no beauty,
And the dust of the soul
    grows thick and unswept;
The spirit is drenched in tears unwept.
But just as we fall beside the road,
Discouraged with life
    and bowed down with our load,
We lift our eyes, and what seemed a dead end
Is the street of dreams where we meet a friend.

Helen Steiner Rice

31
JULY

GIVE MORE, GET MORE

Let not mercy and truth forsake thee:
bind them about thy neck; write them
upon the table of thine heart.

PROVERBS 3:3 KJV

The more you give, the more you get—
The more you laugh, the less you fret.
The more you do unselfishly,
The more you live abundantly—
The more of everything you share,
The more you'll always have to spare.
The more you love, the more you'll find
That life is good and friends are kind,
For only what we give away
Enriches us from day to day.

GOD KNOWS BEST

*Thou shalt love the LORD thy God with all thine heart,
and with all thy soul, and with all thy might.*

DEUTERONOMY 6:5 KJV

With faith in your heart,
    reach out for God's hand
And accept what He sends,
    though you can't understand. . .
For our Father in heaven
    always knows what is best,
And if you trust His wisdom,
    your life will be blessed.

Unfathomable Pleasures

*God will give you everything you need because
of His great riches in Christ Jesus.*

PHILIPPIANS 4:19 NLV

Give Him a chance to open His treasures,
And He'll fill your life
    with unfathomable pleasures—
Pleasures that never grow worn out and faded
And leave us depleted, disillusioned,
    and jaded—
For God has a storehouse
    just filled to the brim
With all that man needs,
    if we'll only ask Him.

One-Minute Meditations

AUGUST 3

LIFT UP YOUR HEAD

*Thou, O Lord, art a shield for me; my glory,
and the lifter up of mine head.*

PSALM 3:3 KJV

May peace and understanding
Give you strength and courage, too,
And may the hours and days ahead
Hold a new hope for you;
For the sorrow that is yours today
Will pass away and then
You'll find the sun of happiness
Will shine for you again.

Helen Steiner Rice

4
AUGUST

Dwelling in God's House

*One thing have I asked of the LORD, that will I seek
after; that I may dwell in the house of the LORD
all the days of my life, to behold the beauty of
the LORD, and to inquire in his temple.*

PSALM 27:4 RSV

Help me when I falter,
Hear me when I pray,
Receive me in Thy kingdom
To dwell with Thee someday.

5
AUGUST

UNEXPECTED MIRACLES

Remember to do good and help each other.
Gifts like this please God.

HEBREWS 13:16 NLV

The unexpected kindness
from an unexpected place,
A hand outstretched in friendship,
a smile on someone's face,
A word of understanding spoken
in a time of trial
Are unexpected miracles that
make life more worthwhile.

Helen Steiner Rice

6
AUGUST

RESURRECTION

Rise up, come to our help!
Deliver us for the sake of thy steadfast love!

PSALM 44:26 RSV

In the resurrection
That takes place in nature's sod,
Let us understand more fully
The risen Savior, Son of God.

A MOTHER'S LOVE

Serve one another in love.

GALATIANS 5:13 NIV

A mother's love is fashioned
After God's enduring love;
It is endless and unfailing
Like the love of Him above.

Helen Steiner Rice

8

AUGUST

A REASON FOR EVERYTHING

*No discipline is enjoyable while it is happening—
it's painful! But afterward there will be a peaceful harvest
of right living for those who are trained in this way.*

HEBREWS 12:11 NLT

Our Father loves His children
    and to Him all things are plain;
He never sends us pleasure
    when the soul's deep need is pain.
So whenever we are troubled
    and when everything goes wrong,
It is just God working in us
    to make our spirits strong.

One-Minute Meditations

9

AUGUST

Look to the Son

*On the day I called, thou didst answer me,
my strength of soul thou didst increase.*

PSALM 138:3 RSV

Most of the battles of life are won
By looking beyond the clouds to the sun.
And having the patience to wait for the day
When the sun comes out and the
clouds float away!

Helen Steiner Rice

10
AUGUST

No Burden Too Heavy

*"Take my yoke upon you, and learn from me;
for I am gentle and lowly in heart, and you
will find rest for your souls. For my yoke
is easy, and my burden is light."*

MATTHEW 11:29–30 RSV

No one ever sought the Father
And found He was not there,
And no burden is too heavy
To be lightened by a prayer.

One-Minute Meditations

11
AUGUST

Included in God's Love

Let your face shine on your servant;
save me in your unfailing love.

PSALM 31:16 NIV

God's love knows no exceptions,
So never feel excluded—
No matter who or what you are,
Your name has been included.

Let All Creation Praise Him

Let them praise the name of the Lord!
For he commanded and they were created.
And he established them for ever and ever;
he fixed their bounds which cannot be passed.

Psalm I48:5–6 rsv

Our Father made the heavens,
The mountains and the hills,
The rivers and the oceans,
And the singing whippoorwills.

SEND ME!

I heard the voice of the Lord saying,
"Whom shall I send, and who will go for us?"
Then I said, "Here am I! Send me."

ISAIAH 6:8 RSV

Hour by hour and day by day
I talk to God and say when I pray,
"God, show me the way so I know what to do;
I am willing and ready if I just knew."

CONNECTED TO THE VINE

"I am the true vine, and my Father is the vinedresser.
Every branch of mine that bears no fruit, he takes away,
and every branch that does bear fruit he prunes,
that it may bear more fruit."

JOHN 15:1–2 RSV

When we cut ourselves away
From guidance that's divine,
Our lives will be as fruitless as
The branch without the vine.

OUR CROSS TO BEAR

*[Jesus] said to all, "If any man would come
after me, let him deny himself and take
up his cross daily and follow me."*

LUKE 9:23 RSV

Everyone has problems
In this restless world of care;
Everyone grows weary
With the cross they have to bear.

Helen Steiner Rice

16
AUGUST

WINGS OF PRAYER

"Therefore I tell you, whatever you ask for in prayer,
believe that you have received it, and it will be yours."

MARK 11:24 NIV

Like a soaring eagle,
You too can rise above
The storms of life around you
On the wings of prayer and love.

17
AUGUST

SINCERE SUPPLICATION

Praying always with all prayer and supplication
in the Spirit, and watching thereunto with all
perseverance and supplication for all saints.

EPHESIANS 6:18 KJV

Often during a busy day
I pause for a minute to silently pray,
I mention the names of those I love
And treasured friends I am fondest of—
For it doesn't matter where we pray
If we honestly mean the words we say,
For God is always listening to hear
The prayers that are made
    by a heart that's sincere.

GOD OUR HELPER

*The Lord is my helper, and I will not
fear what man shall do unto me.*

HEBREWS 13:6 KJV

With God on your side, it matters not who
Is working to keep life's good things from you,
For you need nothing more
    than God's guidance and love
To ensure you the things
    that you're most worthy of.

One-Minute Meditations

19 AUGUST

RENEWAL

*I have no greater joy than to hear that
my children are walking in the truth.*

3 JOHN 1:4 NIV

You are ushering in another day,
    untouched and freshly new,
So here I am to ask You, God,
    if You'll renew me, too. . .
Forgive the many errors that I made yesterday
And let me try again, dear God,
    to walk closer in Thy way. . .
But, Father, I am well aware
    I can't make it on my own,
So take my hand and hold it tight,
    for I can't walk alone.

A PLACE PREPARED

In my Father's house are many mansions: if it were not so, I would have told you. I go to prepare a place for you. And if I go and prepare a place for you, I will come again, and receive you unto myself; that where I am, there ye may be also.

JOHN 14:2–3 KJV

Death is just a natural thing,
    like the closing of a door
As we start up on a journey
    to a new and distant shore. . .
And none need make this journey
    undirected or alone,
For God promised us safe passage
    to this vast and great unknown.

THE GREATEST LOVE

This is my commandment, that ye love one another,
as I have loved you. Greater love hath no man than this,
that a man lay down his life for his friends.

JOHN 15:12–13 KJV

Where there is love the heart is light,
Where there is love the day is bright.
Where there is love there is a song
To help when things are going wrong.

GRACE TO OVERCOME

Now our Lord Jesus Christ himself, and God,
even our Father, which hath loved us, and hath given
us everlasting consolation and good hope through grace. . .

2 THESSALONIANS 2:16 KJV

Blessed are the people who learn to accept
The trouble men try to escape and reject,
For in accordance we're given great grace
And courage and faith and strength to face
The daily troubles that come to us all,
So we may learn to stand straight and tall. . .
For the grandeur of life is born of defeat,
For in overcoming we make life complete.

God Is Good

*The LORD is good, a strong hold in the day of trouble;
and he knoweth them that trust in him.*

NAHUM 1:7 KJV

There are always two sides—
    the good and the bad,
The dark and the light,
    the sad and the glad. . .
But in looking back over
    the good and the bad,
We're aware of the number
    of good things we've had—
And in counting our blessings,
    we find when we're through
We've no reason at all to complain or be blue.

Helen Steiner Rice

24
AUGUST

STRENGTHENED THROUGH STRUGGLES

Cast thy burden upon the LORD, and he shall sustain thee:
he shall never suffer the righteous to be moved.

PSALM 55:22 KJV

Praise God for trouble that cuts like a knife
And disappointments that shatter your life,
For God is but testing
    your faith and your love
Before He appoints you to rise far above
All the small things that so sorely distress you,
For God's only intention
    is to strengthen and bless you.

HEART HUNGER

Behold, I am with thee, and will keep thee in all places whither thou goest, and will bring thee again into this land; for I will not leave thee, until I have done that which I have spoken to thee of.

GENESIS 28:15 KJV

He lived in a palace on a mountain of gold,
Surrounded by riches and wealth untold,
Priceless possessions and treasures of art,
But he died alone of a hungry heart.
For man cannot live by bread alone
No matter what he may have or own.

Helen Steiner Rice

26
AUGUST

MOVER OF MOUNTAINS

*Looking unto Jesus the author and finisher of our faith;
who for the joy that was set before him endured
the cross, despising the shame, and is set down
at the right hand of the throne of God.*

HEBREWS 12:2 KJV

Faith is a force that is greater
    than knowledge or power or skill,
And the darkest defeat turns to triumph
    if you trust in God's wisdom and will,
For faith is a mover of mountains—
    there's nothing man cannot achieve
If he has the courage to try it
    and then has the faith to believe.

SWEET KINDNESS

*"This is what the LORD Almighty says:
'Administer true justice; show mercy
and compassion to one another.'"*

ZECHARIAH 7:9 NIV

There is no garden so complete
But roses could make the place more sweet.
There is no life so rich and rare
But one more friend could enter there.
Like roses in a garden, kindness fills the air
With a certain sweetness
   as it touches everywhere.

GATEWAY TO REWARD

*Because Jesus was raised from the dead, we've been
given a brand-new life and have everything to
live for, including a future in heaven.*

1 PETER 1:3 MSG

Growing older only means
The spirit grows serene
And we behold things with our souls
That our eyes have never seen.
For each birthday is a gateway
That leads to a reward,
The rich reward of learning
The true greatness of the Lord.

29
AUGUST

BLESS AND BE BLESSED

Cast your bread upon the waters,
for you will find it after many days.

ECCLESIASTES 11:1 RSV

You can't pluck a rose
All fragrant with dew
Without part of its fragrance
Remaining with you.

30
AUGUST

Trials Make Us Tough

In the world ye shall have tribulation:
but be of good cheer; I have overcome the world.

JOHN 16:33 KJV

Things achieved too easily
     lose their charm and meaning, too,
For it is life's difficulties
     and the trial times we go through
That make us strong in spirit
     and endow us with the will
To surmount the insurmountable
     and to climb the highest hill.

FORGIVENESS—PASS IT ON!

*For if ye forgive men their trespasses,
your heavenly Father will also forgive you.*

MATTHEW 6:14 KJV

Men may misjudge you,
    but God's verdict is fair,
For He looks deep inside and is deeply aware
Of every small detail in your pattern of living,
And always He's fair and
    lenient and forgiving.

Helen Steiner Rice

I

SEPTEMBER

UNFETTERED HAPPINESS

We are happy for the hope we have of
sharing the shining-greatness of God.

ROMANS 4:2 NLV

Across the years, we've met in dreams
And shared each other's hopes and schemes.
We've known a friendship rich and rare
And beautiful beyond compare. . .
But you reached out your arms for more
To catch what you were yearning for,
But little did you think or guess
That one can't capture happiness
Because it's unrestrained and free,
Unfettered by reality.

2
SEPTEMBER

HELP FROM ABOVE

Is any among you afflicted? let him pray.
Is any merry? let him sing psalms.

JAMES 5:13 KJV

God seems much closer
   and needed much more
When trouble and sorrow
   stand outside our door,
For then we seek shelter in His wondrous love,
And we ask Him to send us help from above.

Helen Steiner Rice

3
SEPTEMBER

WITH US WHEREVER WE GO

I am with thee, and no man shall set on thee to hurt thee:
for I have much people in this city.

ACTS 18:10 KJV

Somebody cares and always will—
The world forgets, but God loves you still.
For God forgives until the end—
He is your faithful, loyal friend.

4

SEPTEMBER

MYSTERIOUS WONDERS

*Blessed be the God and Father of our Lord Jesus
Christ, who hath blessed us with all spiritual
blessings in heavenly places in Christ.*

EPHESIANS 1:3 KJV

In the beauty of a snowflake
  falling softly on the land
Is the mystery and the miracle
  of God's great, creative hand.
What better answers are there
  to prove His holy being
Than the wonders all around us
  that are ours just for the seeing?

Helen Steiner Rice

5
SEPTEMBER

LIFE'S MEASURE

*His mercy is on them that fear him
from generation to generation.*

LUKE 1:50 KJV

We know life's never measured
By how many years we live
But by the kindly things we do
And the happiness we give.

HOPING AND WAITING

It is good that a man should both hope and quietly wait for the salvation of the LORD.

LAMENTATIONS 3:26 KJV

When the waves of tribulation
    seem to drown us in despair,
God's love is like a harbor
    where our souls can find sweet rest
From the struggle and the tension
    of life's fast and futile quest.
God's love is like a beacon
    burning bright with faith and prayer,
And through the changing scenes of life,
    we can find a haven there.

Helen Steiner Rice

SEPTEMBER

TRIUMPH OVER TEMPTATION

*There hath no temptation taken you but such as
is common to man: but God is faithful, who will
not suffer you to be tempted above that ye are able;
but will with the temptation also make a way
to escape, that ye may be able to bear it.*

1 CORINTHIANS 10:13 KJV

Thank God for the good things
   He has already done,
And be grateful to Him
   for the battles you've won—
And know that the same God
   who helped you before
Is ready and willing to help you once more.

LAND OF NO NIGHT

There will be no night [in heaven].
There will be no need for a light of for the sun
because the Lord God will be their light.

REVELATION 22:5 NLV

Into His hands each night as I sleep
I commend my soul for the dear Lord to keep,
Knowing that if my soul should take flight,
It will soar to the land where there is no night.

A Prayer for Mothers

*Herein is love, not that we loved God,
but that he loved us, and sent his Son
to be the propitiation for our sins.*

1 John 4:10 kjv

Our Father in heaven, whose love is divine,
Thanks for the love of a mother like mine.
In Thy great mercy look down from above
And grant this dear mother
    the gift of Your love.

A Sure Inheritance

To an inheritance incorruptible, and undefiled,
and that fadeth not away, reserved in heaven for you. . .

1 PETER 1:4 KJV

While we can't see what's on death's other side,
We know that our Father will richly provide
All that He promised to those who believe,
And His kingdom is waiting for us to receive.

BEAUTY EVERYWHERE

I will speak with the voice of thanks,
and tell of all Your great works.

PSALM 26:7 NLV

Thank You, God, for the beauty
    around me everywhere,
The gentle rain and glistening dew,
    the sunshine and the air,
The joyous gift of feeling
    the soul's soft, whispering voice
That speaks to me from deep within
    and makes my heart rejoice.

COMFORT FOR TODAY, STRENGTH FOR TOMORROW

May [God] give your hearts comfort and strength to say and do every good thing.

2 THESSALONIANS 2:17 NLV

God has told us that nothing can sever
A life He created to live forever.
So let God's promise soften our sorrow
And give us new strength
    for a brighter tomorrow.

Helen Steiner Rice

13
SEPTEMBER

ETERNAL HOME

*For we know that if our earthly house of this
tabernacle were dissolved, we have a building of God,
an house not made with hands, eternal in the heavens.*

2 CORINTHIANS 5:1 KJV

Trust God's all-wise wisdom
And doubt the Father never,
For in His heavenly kingdom
There is nothing lost forever.

THE GOLDEN CHAIN
OF FRIENDSHIP

And [add] to godliness brotherly kindness;
and to brotherly kindness charity.

2 PETER 1:7 KJV

Friendship is a priceless gift
    that can't be bought or sold,
And to have an understanding friend
    is worth far more than gold. . .
And the golden chain of friendship
    is a strong and blessed tie
Binding kindred hearts together
    as the years go passing by.

LOOK AND LISTEN

*"You will look for the Lord your God.
And you will find Him if you look for
Him with all your heart and soul."*

DEUTERONOMY 4:29 NLV

Everywhere across the land
You see God's face and touch His hand.
Each time you look up in the sky
Or watch the fluffy clouds drift by. . .
Or touch a leaf or see a tree,
It's all God whispering, "This is Me. . .
And I am faith and I am light
And in Me there shall be no night."

Ask, Seek, Knock

Ask, and it shall be given you; seek, and ye shall find;
knock, and it shall be opened unto you.

MATTHEW 7:7 KJV

He hears every prayer and answers each one
When we pray in His name,
  "Thy will be done."
And the burdens that seemed
  too heavy to bear
Are lifted away on the wings of prayer.

HOUSEHOLD OF FAITH

*As we have therefore opportunity, let us do good
unto all men, especially unto them who
are of the household of faith.*

GALATIANS 6:10 KJV

Like ships upon the sea of life
We meet with friends so dear,
Then sail on swiftly from the ones
We'd like to linger near;
Sometimes I wish
The winds would cease,
The waves be quiet, too,
And let me sort of drift along
Beside a friend like you.

UPHELD WITH HIS HAND

*Though he fall, he shall not be utterly cast down:
for the LORD upholdeth him with his hand.*

PSALM 37:24 KJV

He's ever present and always there
To take you in His tender care
And bind the wounds and mend the breaks
When all the world around forsakes.
Somebody cares and loves you still,
And God is the Someone who always will.

Helen Steiner Rice

19
SEPTEMBER

A JOYOUS TRANSITION

_My sheep hear my voice,
and I know them, and they follow me._

JOHN 10:27 KJV

Death is not sad—it's time for elation,
A joyous transition, the soul's emigration
Into a place where the soul's safe and free
To live with God through eternity.

PATIENCE TO PERSEVERE

*You need to persevere so that when you have done
the will of God, you will receive what he has promised.*

HEBREWS 10:36 NIV

Most of the battles of life are won
By looking beyond the clouds to the sun
And having the patience to wait for the day
When the sun comes out
    and the clouds float away.

Helen Steiner Rice

21
SEPTEMBER

GOD'S LOVE

God demonstrates his own love for us in this:
While we were still sinners, Christ died for us.

ROMANS 5:8 NIV

God's love is like a sanctuary
    where our souls can find sweet rest
From the struggle and the tension
    of life's fast and futile quest.
God's love is like a tower
    rising far above the crowd,
And God's smile is like the sunshine
    breaking through the threatening cloud.

One-Minute Meditations

22

SEPTEMBER

LOVE—PRICELESS

*Be kindly affectioned one to another with
brotherly love; in honour preferring one another.*

ROMANS 12:10 KJV

The priceless gift of life is love,
For with the help of God above
Love can change the human race
And make this world a better place. . .
For love dissolves all hate and fear
And makes our vision bright and clear
So we can see and rise above
Our pettiness on wings of love.

Helen Steiner Rice

23
SEPTEMBER

JOURNEY ON

*Henceforth there is laid up for me a crown of
righteousness, which the Lord, the righteous judge,
shall give me at that day: and not to me only,
but unto all them also that love his appearing.*

2 TIMOTHY 4:8 KJV

Nothing is ever too hard to do
If your faith is strong
    and your purpose is true. . .
So never give up, and never stop—
Just journey on to the mountaintop!

One-Minute Meditations

24
SEPTEMBER

COUNT YOUR BLESSINGS

Blessed are they which do hunger and thirst after
righteousness: for they shall be filled.

MATTHEW 5:6 KJV

Happiness is something
    we create in our minds—
It's not something you search for
    and so seldom find.
It's just waking up and beginning the day
By counting our blessings
    and kneeling to pray.

Helen Steiner Rice

25
SEPTEMBER

SILENT RENEWAL

*He washed away our sins, giving us a new
birth and new life through the Holy Spirit.*

TITUS 3:5 NLT

Silently the green leaves grow,
In silence falls the soft white snow,
Silently the flowers bloom,
In silence sunshine fills a room—
Silently bright stars appear,
In silence velvet night draws near,
And silently God enters in
To free a troubled heart from sin. . .
For God works silently in lives.

26

SEPTEMBER

FAITH TO PERSEVERE

*Let us run with perseverance
the race marked out for us.*

HEBREWS 12:1 NIV

Although it sometimes seems to us
    our prayers have not been heard,
God always knows our every need
    without a single word,
And He will not forsake us
    even though the way is steep,
For always He is near to us,
    a tender watch to keep.

Helen Steiner Rice

27
SEPTEMBER

No Fear

"See, God saves me. I will trust and not be afraid.
For the Lord God is my strength and song."

ISAIAH 12:2 NLV

Suddenly, Lord, I'm no longer afraid—
My burden is lighter
and the dark shadows fade.
Oh God, what a comfort
to know that You care
And to know when I seek You,
You will always be there.

28
SEPTEMBER

UNFLAPPABLE FAITH

*Now faith is being sure of what we hope
for and certain of what we do not see.*

HEBREWS 11:1 NIV

Secure is that blessed assurance,
We can smile as we face tomorrow,
For God holds the key to the future,
And no sorrow or care we need borrow.

OPEN MY EYES, LORD

The eyes of the Lord are over the righteous,
and his ears are open unto their prayers: but the
face of the Lord is against them that do evil.

1 PETER 3:12 KJV

God, open my eyes so I may see
And feel Your presence close to me.
Give me strength for my stumbling feet
As I battle the crowd on life's busy street.

30
SEPTEMBER

CHILDREN OF THE HEAVENLY FATHER

*[I] will be a Father unto you, and ye shall be my
sons and daughters, saith the Lord Almighty.*

2 CORINTHIANS 6:18 KJV

I cannot dwell apart from You—
You would not ask or want me to,
For You have room within Your heart
To make each child of Yours a part
Of You and all Your love and care
If we but come to You in prayer.

Prayer—the Best Stress Buster

*There is no wisdom nor understanding
nor counsel against the Lord.*

Proverbs 21:30 KJV

When your nervous network
    becomes a tangled mess,
Just close your eyes in silent prayer
    and ask the Lord to bless
Each thought that you are thinking,
    each decision you must make,
As well as every word you speak
    and every step you take.

One-Minute Meditations

2

OCTOBER

FAITHFUL UNTIL THE END

Bless the LORD, O my soul, and forget not all his benefits,
who forgives all your iniquity. . .who crowns you
with steadfast love and mercy, who satisfies
you with good as long as you live.

PSALM 103:2–5 ESV

God forgives you until the end;
He is your faithful, loyal friend.
Somebody cares and loves you still,
And God is the Someone who always will.

Helen Steiner Rice

3
OCTOBER

PEACE IN GOD'S PRESENCE

*"O my God," I say, "take me not hence
in the midst of my days, thou whose years
endure throughout all generations!"*

PSALM 102:24 RSV

Show us that in quietness
We can feel Your presence near,
Filling us with joy and peace
Throughout the coming year.

LOVE LEADS US HOME

Jesus answered him, "If a man loves me, he will keep my word, and my Father will love him, and we will come to him and make our home with him."

JOHN 14:23 RSV

Only love can make man kind,
And kindness of heart brings peace of mind,
And by giving love we can start this year
To lift the clouds of hate and fear.

CLOSE TO GOD'S HEART

The LORD is near to the brokenhearted,
and saves the crushed in spirit.

PSALM 34:18 ESV

May He who hears our every prayer
Keep you in His loving care—
And may you feel His presence near
Each day throughout the coming year.

6

OCTOBER

Flowering Friendship

*"Their life shall be like a watered garden,
and they shall languish no more."*

JEREMIAH 31:12 RSV

Friendship, like flowers,
Blooms ever more fair
When carefully tended
By dear friends who care.

Helen Steiner Rice

7
OCTOBER

Reveal Your Will, O God

This is the confidence which we have in him,
that if we ask anything according to his will he hears us.

1 JOHN 5:14 RSV

Teach me to let go, dear God,
And pray undisturbed until
My heart is filled with inner peace
And I learn to know Your will!

8

OCTOBER

SHEPHERD OF OUR HEARTS

*"I am the door; if any one enters by me, he will be saved,
and will go in and out and find pasture."*

JOHN 10:9 RSV

Open your heart's door
    and let Christ come in,
And He will give you new life
    and free you from sin,
And there is no joy that can ever compare
With the joy of knowing you're in God's care.

Helen Steiner Rice

9

OCTOBER

GOD'S HAND IS EVERYWHERE

*Arise, L*ORD*! Lift up your hand, O God.*
Do not forget the helpless.

PSALM 10:12 NIV

It's true we have never looked on His face,
But His likeness shines forth from every place,
For the hand of God is everywhere
Along life's busy thoroughfare,
And His presence can be felt and seen
Right in the midst of our daily routine.

THE SUNLIGHT OF GOD'S DAY

"Truly, truly, I say to you, the hour is coming,
and now is, when the dead will hear the voice of
the Son of God, and those who hear will live."

JOHN 5:25 RSV

Flowers sleep beneath the ground,
But when they hear spring's waking sound,
They push themselves through layers of clay
To reach the sunlight of God's day.

UNFAILING PROMISES

Keep your life free from love of money, and be
content with what you have; for he has said,
"I will never fail you nor forsake you."

HEBREWS 13:5 RSV

Know that the promises of God
Will never fail or falter,
And you will inherit everlasting life
Which even death cannot alter.

An Attitude of Gratitude

*"As the rain and the snow come down from heaven,
and do not return to it without watering the earth and
making it bud and flourish, so that it yields seed for
the sower and bread for the eater, so is my word
that goes out from my mouth."*

Isaiah 55:10–11 NIV

The good, green earth beneath our feet,
The air we breathe, the food we eat—
All these things and many more
Are things we should be thankful for.

Helen Steiner Rice

13
OCTOBER

PRACTICING GOD'S PRECEPTS

*Finally, brethren, whatever is true, whatever is honorable,
whatever is just, whatever is pure, whatever is lovely,
whatever is gracious, if there is any excellence, if there
is anything worthy of praise, think about these things.
What you have learned and received and heard and seen
in me, do; and the God of peace will be with you.*

PHILIPPIANS 4:8–9 RSV

Give us strength and courage
To be honorable and true,
Practicing Your precepts
In everything we do.

14
OCTOBER

Our Light in Darkness

You, O Lord, keep my lamp burning;
my God turns my darkness into light.

PSALM 18:28 NIV

God did not promise sun without rain,
Light without darkness or joy without pain—
He only promised us strength for the day
When the darkness comes
   and we lose our way.

**15
OCTOBER**

NEVER FEAR—
GOD'S PLANS ARE GOOD

*"For I know the plans I have for you,
says the LORD, plans for welfare and not for evil,
to give you a future and a hope."*

JEREMIAH 29:11 RSV

Remember when you're troubled
With uncertainty and doubt,
It is best to tell your Father
What your fear is all about.

16
OCTOBER

THE CROSS, CHRIST'S TRIUMPH

Having disarmed the powers and authorities,
he made a public spectacle of them,
triumphing over them by the cross.

COLOSSIANS 2:15 NIV

Though we grow discouraged
In this world we're living in,
There is comfort just in knowing
God has triumphed over sin.

17
OCTOBER

OUR SOVEREIGN GOD

I will come and proclaim your mighty acts,
O Sovereign LORD; I will proclaim
your righteousness, yours alone.

PSALM 71:16 NIV

God, make us conscious
That Your love comes in many ways,
And not always just as happiness
And bright and shining days.

INFINITE BLESSINGS

He will receive blessing from the LORD,
and vindication from the God of his salvation.

PSALM 24:5 RSV

No matter how big man's dreams are,
God's blessings are infinitely more,
For always God's giving is greater
Than what man is asking for.

ADD A LITTLE SUNSHINE

*If your enemy is hungry, give him bread to eat;
and if he is thirsty, give him water to drink.*

PROVERBS 25:21 RSV

To live a little better,
Always be forgiving.
Add a little sunshine
To the world in which we're living.

Overtaken by Blessings

*"All these blessings shall come upon you and overtake you,
if you obey the voice of the LORD your God."*

DEUTERONOMY 28:2 RSV

God, renew our spirits
And make us more aware
That our future is dependent
On sacrifice and prayer.

OUR HELP IN TROUBLE

God is our refuge and strength,
a very present help in trouble.

PSALM 46:1 ESV

Above the noise and laughter
That is empty, cruel, and loud,
Do you listen for the voice of God
In the restless, surging crowd?

YOUR WILL, NOT MINE

"I desire to do your will, O my God;
your law is within my heart."

PSALM 40:8 NIV

God hears every prayer,
And He answers each one
When we pray in His name,
"Thy will be done."

Helen Steiner Rice

23
OCTOBER

TAKE COURAGE

*Wait for the LORD; be strong, and let your heart
take courage; yea, wait for the LORD!*

PSALM 27:14 RSV

Grant me faith and courage;
Put purpose in my days.
Show me how to serve Thee
In the most effective ways.

RESTING PLACE

My people will live in peaceful dwelling places,
in secure homes, in undisturbed places of rest.

ISAIAH 32:18 NIV

The road will grow much smoother
And much easier to face,
So do not be disheartened—
This is just a resting place.

Helen Steiner Rice

25
OCTOBER

BLESSINGS IN MANY GUISES

*"The Lord bless you and keep you; the Lord make
his face shine upon you and be gracious to you;
the Lord turn his face toward you and give you peace."*

NUMBERS 6:24–26 NIV

God speaks to us in many ways,
Altering our lives, our plans and days,
And His blessings come in many guises
That He alone in love devises.

Arms Open Wide

*He that spared not his own Son, but delivered
him up for us all, how shall he not with him
also freely give us all things?*

ROMANS 8:32 KJV

There is only one place and only one Friend
Who is never too busy,
    and you can always depend
On Him to be waiting with arms open wide
To hear all the troubles
    you came to confide.

Helen Steiner Rice

27
OCTOBER

STAIRWAY OF PRAYER

My soul will be happy in the Lord.
It will be full of joy because He saves.

PSALM 35:9 NLV

Prayers are the stairs that lead to God,
And there's joy every step of the way
When we make our pilgrimage to Him
With love in our hearts each day.

RECONCILED

*Now then we are ambassadors for Christ, as though
God did beseech you by us: we pray you in Christ's stead,
be ye reconciled to God. For he hath made him to be
sin for us, who knew no sin; that we might
be made the righteousness of God in him.*

2 CORINTHIANS 5:20–21 KJV

God of love, forgive—forgive.
Teach me how to truly live.
Ask me not my race or creed,
Just take me in my hour of need
And let me know You love me, too,
And that I am a part of You.

GUIDED BY HIS HAND

Fear not, O land; be glad and rejoice:
for the LORD will do great things.

JOEL 2:21 KJV

There are many things in life
  we cannot understand,
But we must trust God's judgment
  and be guided by His hand. . .
And all who have God's blessing
  can rest safely in His care,
For He promises safe passage
  on the wings of faith and prayer.

THE RICHEST REWARD

*The man who plants and the man who
waters have one purpose, and each will be
rewarded according to his own labor.*

1 CORINTHIANS 3:8 NIV

Let me be great
In the eyes of the Lord,
For that is the richest,
Most priceless reward.

Helen Steiner Rice

31
OCTOBER

LEAVE TOMORROW TO GOD

There is a future for the man of peace.

PSALM 37:37 NIV

Forget the past and future
And dwell wholly on today,
For God controls the future,
And He will direct our way.

SACRIFICIAL LOVE

Her children rise up and call her blessed;
her husband also, and he praises her.

PROVERBS 31:28 ESV

A mother's love is something
That no one can explain;
It is made of deep devotion
And of sacrifice and pain.

Helen Steiner Rice

2
NOVEMBER

SHINE YOUR LIGHT

"You are my lamp, O LORD;
the LORD turns my darkness into light."

2 SAMUEL 22:29 NIV

The Lord is our salvation
And our strength in every fight,
Our redeemer and protector,
Our eternal guiding light. . .
He has promised to sustain us,
He's our refuge from all harms,
And underneath this refuge
Are the everlasting arms.

3
NOVEMBER

ENDLESS LOVE

For the wages of sin is death,
but the free gift of God is eternal life
in Christ Jesus our Lord.

ROMANS 6:23 RSV

To know life is unending
And God's love is endless, too,
Makes our daily tasks and burdens
So much easier to do.

Helen Steiner Rice

DIVINE ASSISTANCE

Surely there is a future, and your hope will not be cut off.

PROVERBS 23:18 RSV

Our future will seem brighter
And we'll meet with less resistance
If we call upon our Father
And seek divine assistance.

GOD'S MIGHTY, MERCIFUL LOVE

Have mercy on me, O God, according to your unfailing love; according to your great compassion blot out my transgressions.

PSALM 51:1 NIV

I am perplexed and often vexed,
And sometimes I cry and sadly sigh,
But do not think, dear Father above,
I question You or Your unchanging love.

LITTLE GIFTS

The steps of a man are from the LORD,
and he establishes him in whose way he delights.

PSALM 37:23 RSV

Every happy happening
And every lucky break
Are little gifts from God above
That are ours to freely take.

THE GREATNESS OF LOVE

So faith, hope, love abide, these three;
but the greatest of these is love.

1 CORINTHIANS 13:13 RSV

Where there is love, there is a smile
To make all things seem more worthwhile;
Where there is love, there's a quiet peace,
A tranquil place where turmoils cease.

Helen Steiner Rice

8

NOVEMBER

A Cheerful Heart

A cheerful heart is a good medicine.

PROVERBS 17:22 RSV

If you'll only try to be cheerful,
You will find, without a doubt,
A cheerful attitude is something
No one should be without.

One-Minute Meditations

9
NOVEMBER

HE HOLDS MY HAND

"I, the LORD, have called you in righteousness;
I will take hold of your hand."

ISAIAH 42:6 NIV

Take the Savior's loving hand
And do not try to understand;
Just let Him lead you where He will
Through pastures green, by waters still.

Helen Steiner Rice

10
NOVEMBER

STRONG CONFIDENCE

*In the fear of the LORD one has strong confidence,
and his children will have a refuge.*

PROVERBS 14:26 RSV

There's a lot of comfort in the thought
That sorrow, grief, and woe
Are sent into our lives sometimes
To help our souls to grow.

11

NOVEMBER

LITTLE THINGS

*Better is a little with righteousness
than great revenues with injustice.*

PROVERBS 16:8 RSV

Thank You, God, for little things
That often come our way—
The things we take for granted
But don't mention when we pray.

GOD'S PRESENCE MAKES GLAD

"Thou hast made known to me the ways of life;
thou wilt make me full of gladness with thy presence."

ACTS 2:28 RSV

Keep looking for an angel
And keep listening to hear,
For on life's busy, crowded streets,
You will find God's presence near.

One-Minute Meditations

PERFECT LOVE

The LORD is gracious and compassionate,
slow to anger and rich in love.

PSALM 145:8 NIV

Wonder of wonders,
Beyond man's conception,
For only in God
Can love find true perfection.

THANK GOD!

*It is good to give thanks to the LORD, to sing praises to
thy name, O Most High; to declare thy steadfast love
in the morning, and thy faithfulness by night.*

PSALM 92:1–2 RSV

Thank You, God, for little things
That come unexpectedly
To brighten up a dreary day
That dawned so dismally.

MEDITATE ON GOD'S GOODNESS

May my meditation be pleasing to him,
for I rejoice in the LORD.

PSALM 104:34 RSV

When your day is pressure-packed
And your hours are all too few,
Just close your eyes and meditate
And let God talk to you.

TAKE TIME TO BE KIND

*Always try to be kind to each other
and to everyone else.*

1 THESSALONIANS 5:15 NIV

In this troubled world
It's refreshing to find
Someone who still
Has the time to be kind.

GOD'S PROMISES ARE FOREVER

This is what he promised us—
even eternal life.

1 JOHN 2:25 NIV

When God makes a promise,
It remains forever true,
For everything God promises,
He unalterably will do.

IN HIM WE LIVE

*As soon as Jesus heard the word that was spoken,
he saith unto the ruler of the synagogue,
Be not afraid, only believe.*

MARK 5:36 KJV

Life's a mystery man can't understand,
The great giver of life is holding our hands,
And safe in His care
  there is no need for seeing,
"For in Him we live and move
  and have our being."

19
NOVEMBER

ABUNDANT BLESSINGS

Blessed are the pure in heart: for they shall see God.

MATTHEW 5:8 KJV

Love alone can make us kind
And give us joy and peace of mind,
So live with joy unselfishly
And you'll be blessed abundantly.

20
NOVEMBER

ETERNAL DAY

*Nevertheless we, according to his promise,
look for new heavens and a new earth,
wherein dwelleth righteousness.*

2 PETER 3:13 KJV

If you are searching to find the way
To life everlasting and eternal day,
With faith in your heart
      take the path that He trod,
For the way of the cross is the way to God.

THE LIFE AND THE LIGHT

[Jesus Christ] is gone into heaven,
and is on the right hand of God; angels and authorities
and powers being made subject unto him.

1 PETER 3:22 KJV

I am the Life, and I hold the key
That opens the door to eternity. . .
And in this dark world, I am the Light
To the promised land where there is no night.

SHOW ME THE WAY

Blessed is he that considereth the poor: the LORD will deliver him in time of trouble.

PSALM 41:1 KJV

No one discovers the fullness
Or the greatness of God's love
Unless they have walked in the darkness
With only a light from above.

One-Minute Meditations

23
NOVEMBER

PRICELESS GIFTS

A good name is to be chosen rather than great riches,
and favor is better than silver or gold.

PROVERBS 22:1 RSV

When you ask God for a gift,
Be thankful if He sends
Not diamonds, pearls, or riches,
But the love of real true friends.

JUST DO YOUR BEST

*Be doers of the word,
and not hearers only, deceiving yourselves.*

JAMES 1:22 RSV

God only asks us
To do our best;
Then He will take over
And finish the rest.

GREEN PASTURES

*Know that the LORD is God! It is he that made us,
and we are his; we are his people,
and the sheep of his pasture.*

PSALM 100:3 RSV

For as the flowering branches
Depend upon the tree
To nourish and fulfill them
Till they reach their futurity,
We, too, must be dependent
On our Father above,
For we are but the branches
And He's the tree of love.

Helen Steiner Rice

26
NOVEMBER

Pursue Kindness

*He who pursues righteousness and
kindness will find life and honor.*

PROVERBS 21:21 RSV

If you practice kindness
In all you say and do,
The Lord will wrap His kindness
Around your heart and you.

GOD'S FAITHFUL LOVE

The LORD will work out his plans for my life—
for your faithful love, O LORD, endures forever.
Don't abandon me, for you made me.

PSALM 138:8 NLT

God's love endures forever—
What a wonderful thing to know
When the tides of life run against you
And your spirit is downcast and low.

BLESS THIS HOUSE

*The LORD's curse is on the house of the wicked,
but he blesses the home of the righteous.*

PROVERBS 3:33 NIV

Dear God, let Thy peace be over all;
Let it hang from every wall.
Bless this house with joy and love;
Watch it from Your home above.
Bless this house and may it be
Forever in the care of Thee.

No Hills Too High

*I lift up my eyes to the hills—where does my help
come from? My help comes from the LORD,
the Maker of heaven and earth.*

PSALM 121:1–2 NIV

Life is a highway
On which the years go by—
Sometimes the road is level;
Sometimes the hills are high.

Helen Steiner Rice

30
NOVEMBER

FRESH COURAGE

*Be strong, and let your heart take courage,
all you who wait for the LORD!*

PSALM 31:24 ESV

God, grant me courage
   and hope for every day,
Faith to guide me along my way,
Understanding and wisdom, too,
And grace to accept what life gives me to do.

Pop-Up Prayers

The LORD has heard my supplication;
the LORD will receive my prayer.

PSALM 6:9 KJV

Often during a busy day,
Pause for a minute and silently pray;
Mention the names of those you love
And treasured friends you're fondest of.

Helen Steiner Rice

2
DECEMBER

No Complaints

Do everything without complaining or arguing.

PHILIPPIANS 2:14 NIV

Our Father knows what's best for us,
So why should we complain?
We always want the sunshine,
But He knows there must be rain.

Spring Winds

*So we do not lose heart. Though our outer
nature is wasting away, our inner nature
is being renewed every day.*

2 Corinthians 4:16 RSV

Flowers sleeping peacefully
Beneath the winter's snow
Awaken from their icy grave
When spring winds start to blow.

Helen Steiner Rice

4
DECEMBER

TENDER MEMORIES

The righteous will never be moved;
he will be remembered for ever.

PSALM 112:6 RSV

Tender little memories
Of some word or deed
Give us strength and courage
When we are in need.

5

DECEMBER

PEACE TO GOD'S PEOPLE

*Let me hear what God the LORD will speak,
for he will speak peace to his people, to his saints,
to those who turn to him in their hearts.*

PSALM 85:8 RSV

By keeping Christ in Christmas
We are helping to fulfill
The glad tidings of the angels—
"Peace on earth and to men goodwill."

LOVE ONE ANOTHER

This is the message you heard from the beginning:
We should love one another.

1 JOHN 3:11 NIV

The priceless gift of life is love,
For with the help of God above,
Love can change the human race
And make this world a better place.

7

DECEMBER

THE MIRACLE OF CHRISTMAS

*I will give to the LORD the thanks due to his
righteousness, and I will sing praise to
the name of the LORD, the Most High.*

PSALM 7:17 RSV

Miracles are marvels
That defy all explanation,
And Christmas is a miracle
And not just a celebration.

As the Wind Blows

*[God said,] "I've called your name.
You're mine."*

ISAIAH 43:4 MSG

God is no stranger in a faraway place—
He's as close as the wind
    that blows 'cross my face.
It's true I can't see the wind as it blows,
But I feel it around me
    and my heart surely knows
That God's mighty hand
    can be felt everywhere,
For there's nothing on earth
    that is not in God's care.

9
DECEMBER

BLESSED IS THE GIVER

Every man shall give as he is able,
according to the blessing of the LORD
thy God which he hath given thee.

DEUTERONOMY 16:17 KJV

A kind and thoughtful deed
Or a hand outstretched in a time of need
Is the rarest of gifts, for it is a part
Not of the purse but of a loving heart. . .
And he who gives of himself will find
True joy of heart and peace of mind.

Helen Steiner Rice

10
DECEMBER

THE PROMISE OF CHRISTMAS

*Not to us, O LORD, not to us,
but to thy name give glory, for the sake of
thy steadfast love and thy faithfulness!*

PSALM 115:1 RSV

Make us aware
That the Christmas story
Is everyone's promise
Of eternal glory.

REBIRTH

But when thou makest a feast, call the poor, the maimed,
the lame, the blind: And thou shalt be blessed;
for they cannot recompense thee: for thou shalt be
recompensed at the resurrection of the just.

LUKE 14:13–14 KJV

Oh, give us faith to believe again
That peace on earth, goodwill to men
Will follow this winter of man's mind
And awaken his heart and make him kind. . .
And just as great nature sends the spring
To give new birth to each sleeping thing,
God, grant rebirth to man's slumbering soul
And help him forsake his selfish goal.

DAILY GRACES

"[God] has not left himself without testimony: He has shown kindness by giving you rain from heaven and crops in their seasons; he provides you with plenty of food and fills your hearts with joy."

ACTS 14:17 NIV

Oh, make us more aware, dear God,
Of little daily graces
That come to us with sweet surprise
From never-dreamed-of places.

One-Minute Meditations

13 DECEMBER

GOD'S CREATIVE HAND

Praise the LORD from the earth. . .fire and hail,
snow and frost, stormy wind fulfilling his command!

PSALM 148:7–8 RSV

In the beauty of a snowflake,
Falling softly on the land,
Is the mystery and miracle
Of God's great creative hand!

Helen Steiner Rice

14
DECEMBER

LOVE IS A VERB

Beloved, if God so loved us,
we also ought to love one another.

1 JOHN 4:11 RSV

Peace on earth cannot be found
Until we meet on common ground
And every man becomes a brother
Who worships God and loves all others.

GODLY LIVING

*Teaching us that, denying ungodliness
and worldly lusts, we should live soberly,
righteously, and godly, in this present world.*

TITUS 2:12 KJV

"Do justice"—"Love kindness"—
   "Walk humbly with God"—
For with these three things
   as your rule and your rod,
All things worth having are yours to achieve,
If you follow God's words
   and have faith to believe.

FAITH TO BELIEVE

*Let us not be weary in well doing:
for in due season we shall reap, if we faint not.*

GALATIANS 6:9 KJV

It's easy to grow downhearted
    when nothing goes your way,
It's easy to be discouraged
    when you have a troublesome day,
But trouble is only a challenge
    to spur you on to achieve
The best that God has to offer
    if you have the faith to believe!

17
DECEMBER

WARMTH AND WONDERMENT

The unfolding of thy words gives light;
it imparts understanding to the simple.

PSALM 119:130 RSV

May every heart and every home
Continue through the year
To feel the warmth and wonderment
Of this season of good cheer.

Helen Steiner Rice

18
DECEMBER

CHANGING SEASONS

"Blessed be the name of God for ever and ever,
to whom belong wisdom and might.
He changes times and seasons."

DANIEL 2:20–21 RSV

With nothing but sameness
   how dull life would be,
For only life's challenge can set the soul free,
And it takes a mixture of both bitter and sweet
To season our lives and make them complete.

GOD WEIGHS OUR HEARTS

*Every way of a man is right in his own eyes,
but the LORD weighs the heart.*

PROVERBS 21:2 RSV

Teach me to let go, dear God,
And pray undisturbed until
My heart is filled with inner peace
And I learn to know Your will!

Helen Steiner Rice

20
DECEMBER

SILENT COMMUNION

For God alone my soul waits in silence;
from him comes my salvation.

PSALM 62:1 RSV

Kneel in prayer in His presence,
And you'll find no need to speak,
For softly in silent communion,
God grants you the peace that you seek.

HIDDEN MAJESTY

O LORD, our Lord, how majestic
is thy name in all the earth!

PSALM 8:1 RSV

Little do we realize
That the glory and the power
Of Him who made the universe
Lie hidden in a flower.

22
DECEMBER

BOUNDLESS MERCY

*Have mercy on me, O God, according to thy
steadfast love; according to thy abundant
mercy blot out my transgressions.*

PSALM 51:1 RSV

God, I know that I love You,
And I know without doubt
That Your goodness and mercy
Never run out.

23
DECEMBER

HIGHER GOALS

*I press on toward the goal to win the prize for which
God has called me heavenward in Christ Jesus.*

PHILIPPIANS 3:14 NIV

Father up in heaven,
Stir and wake our sleeping souls;
Renew our faith and lift us up
And give us higher goals.

GOD WITH US

*Upon thee was I cast from my birth,
and since my mother bore me thou hast been my God.*

PSALM 22:10 RSV

May the holy remembrance
Of the first Christmas Day
Be our reassurance
Christ is not far away.

GOD'S PATTERN FOR LIVING

*I give thee thanks, O LORD, with my whole heart. . .
for thou hast exalted above everything
thy name and thy word.*

PSALM 138:1–2 RSV

Christmas is more than a day
     at the end of the year,
More than a season of joy and good cheer;
Christmas is really God's pattern for living
To be followed all year by unselfish giving.

WINTER IS NOT FOREVER

*Water will gush forth in the wilderness
and streams in the desert.*

ISAIAH 35:6 NIV

The bleakness of the winter
Is melted by the sun;
The tree that looked so stark and dead
Becomes a living one.

WALKING IN RIGHTEOUSNESS

*"I will walk among you, and will be your God,
and you shall be my people."*

LEVITICUS 26:12 RSV

Here is a prayer for you
That you'll walk with God every day,
Remembering always in whatever you do,
There is only one true righteous way.

28

DECEMBER

How Can I Repay?

How can I repay the LORD for all his goodness to me? . . .
I will fulfill my vows to the LORD.

PSALM 116:12, 14 NIV

Lord, show me the way I can somehow repay
The blessings You've given to me. . .
Lord, teach me to do
   what You most want me to
And to be what You want me to be.

29
DECEMBER

LET GO AND LET GOD

*Trust in the LORD with all your heart, and do not rely
on your own insight. In all your ways acknowledge him,
and he will make straight your paths.*

PROVERBS 3:5–6 RSV

Rest and relax and grow stronger,
Let go and let God share your load;
Your work is not finished or ended,
You've just come to a bend in the road.

Helen Steiner Rice

30
DECEMBER

DON'T BE DISCOURAGED

"Be strong and courageous. Do not be terrified;
do not be discouraged, for the LORD your God
will be with you wherever you go."

JOSHUA 1:9 NIV

My blessings are so many;
My troubles are so few.
How can I feel discouraged
When I know that I have You?

31
DECEMBER

A YEAR OF BLESSINGS

Thou crownest the year with thy bounty.

PSALM 65:11 RSV

Thank You, dear God,
For the year that now ends
And for the great blessing
Of loved ones and friends.

SCRIPTURE INDEX